The Lost Aztec Code

"Marty Matz, akashic wizard and shamanic warrior, gives us a master-piece in song and saga. . . . A revelation for all time!"

IRA COHEN, poet and author of
Poems from the Akashic Record

"Like a shaman throwing light into the deepest recesses of night, John Major Jenkins and Martin Matz poetically illuminate the secret knowledge contained in the Pyramid of Fire. Jenkins and Matz are elucidators and keepers of the rarest flame."

LAKI VAZAKAS, director of the video documentaries
Huncke and Louis and *Burma: Traces of the Buddha*

"Marty Matz is the lost Beat genius and *Pyramid of Fire* is everything from his spiritual autobiography to a classic world text of enlightenment, letting the wisdom of the Aztecs unfold alongside Marty's epic and torturous quest to find meaning in his own life. The juxtaposition of the wisdom of the Aztecs and Marty's stories and memoirs and the commentary of scholar John Major Jenkins gives us a map of the inner resources by which we all may find our way to the same light that guided Marty through such a splendidly fulfilled life."

GERALD NICOSIA, poet and author of
Memory Babe: A Critical Biography of Jack Kerouac

Quetzalcoatl and Mictlantecuhtli, the gods of life and death

Pyramid of Fire:
The Lost Aztec Codex

Spiritual Ascent at the End of Time

John Major Jenkins
and Martin Matz

Bear & Company
Rochester, Vermont

Bear & Company
One Park Street
Rochester, Vermont 05767
www.InnerTraditions.com

LIBRARY OF CONGRESS CATALOGING-IN-PUBLICATION DATA

Jenkins, John Major.
Pyramid of fire : the lost Aztec codex : spiritual ascent at the end of time / John Major Jenkins and Martin Matz.
p. cm.
Includes bibliographical references (p.   ) and index.
ISBN 1-59143-032-1 (pbk.)
1. Spiritual life—Miscellanea. 2. Aztecs—Religion—Miscellanea. 3. Matz, Martin. I. Title: At head of title: Quetzalcoatl and Mictlantecuhti, the gods of life and death. II. Matz, Martin. III. Pyramid of fire. English. IV. Title.
BF1999.J38 2004
299.7'8452—dc22
2004019632

Printed and bound in the United States by Capital City Press

10   9   8   7   6   5   4   3   2   1

Text design by Priscilla Baker
Text layout by Virginia Scott Bowman
This book was typeset in Adobe Garamond with
Runa Serif and Agenda as the display typefaces

Illustration credits: Frontispiece, figure 4.1, and figure 5.5 from Codex Borgia. Figure 1.1 courtesy of Bobby Yarra. Figure 3.2 from *Telos* by Arthur Versluis. Figure 2.2 from *Zapotec* by Helen Auger. Figures 4.2, 4.3, 4.5, 4.6, and top of 4.4 from Codex Borbonicus. Bottom of figure 4.4 from Codex Laud. Figure 5.4, photo by the author.

Contents

Time Waits

Time waits

A sometimes mossy line

Between November and the sea

Time waits

For me alone

Turning slowly from sound of bass and neon solitude

To the two o'clock ache of warm green on the mountain

Time waits

And somewhere

Out beyond the Mexico City blues

Two bird-like hearts

Beat their way

From dream to dream

Searching

For a field of music

In the restless palm of eternity

—Marty Matz

Foreword

"In this world
I chose to wander
from miracle to marvel to wonder
I learned
all things open
and
life indeed unfolds"

MARTY MATZ, "A FUNNY THING HAPPENED ON
MY WAY TO ENLIGHTENMENT"

With Marty miracles were just bound to happen, if for no other reason than he believed in them. One rainy night in New York City sometime in 1993 a friend of ours said, "You must come with me to hear a lecture by Terence McKenna and I will introduce you to him. I think he has some knowledge of the Mayans and Aztecs. He might be interested in the Pyramid of Fire codex. I know he spent quite some time in the Amazon jungles doing medicinal plant research."

We were a bit skeptical about an American "shaman" but were nevertheless curious and went to the lecture with our friend. Once properly introduced, Marty described for Terence the Pyramid of Fire codex and told him how he had acquired it through his friendship with a Mazatec Indian who was a keeper of the ancient wisdom. Terence gave us his home address and phone number in Hawaii and said to be sure to send him a copy of the codex, which we did immediately.

We didn't hear from Terence for quite some time, but then one day sometime in late 1994 he called. He said he had received the codex and found it very interesting and unusual but felt it went beyond his knowledge of such things. He suggested we contact John Major Jenkins, whom he said was quite an expert on Mayan and Aztec history and philosophy. Marty then called John and, indeed, the miracle happened. Here was someone who was a Mayan and Aztec scholar, as well as a mystic, metaphysician, poet, philosopher, and a very talented published author.

After his first conversations with John, Marty was just thrilled. John was the person who at last truly understood the meaning and value of the Pyramid of Fire. The two spent many hours on the phone together talking about the codex and developed a bond such as only like-minded people can. At John's suggestion, we saw that the codex could become a published reality.

Sometime around 1961 Marty was initiated into the secret knowledge contained in the Pyramid of Fire by don Daniel, a Mazatec shaman well up in his years, and then immediately went about making an English translation of it. After transcribing the original pictographic form of the codex, he spent many years guarding it. He read it to a number of poets, but the Pyramid of Fire requires some study, and its wisdom simply cannot be grasped in its entirety in a single reading. I remember some of Marty's fellow poets saying, "Well, that sounds interesting . . . ," but basically they were mystified. The time had not yet come for them to have a genuine interest in a document dealing with such profound spiritual insights.

It is another miracle that Marty managed to hold on to a copy of the codex for such a long time and through so many relocations—some thirty-three years from the time he transcribed it until the time he sent a copy to John. But he knew what was worth saving. As he said in his poem "A Funny Thing Happened on My Way to Enlightenment,"

> *I have never hesitated*
> *to throw away my wallet*
> *to make room in my pockets for poems or*
> *rainbows*
> *which I carried*

till the rainbows turned
to tattered colors
and the poems
became just dust.*

When I first met Marty I knew I had run into a special genius and offered to type up anything he needed. And so came the task of typing and organizing writings from his rolled up, dirty, tattered, coffee- and wine-stained notebook pages. He was very angry with himself because he couldn't find the thirteenth page of the codex, which was not so surprising to me. Everything Marty had written that was not stuck to a wall somewhere or left for others to find beneath a rock in the mountains of Mexico, Central, or South America, was stuffed into his backpack, a disintegrating sack as ragged as his copy of the codex. He was delighted that I could put the surviving pages of the codex into printed form, and I felt I was serving to preserve the knowledge of humankind. We were married in 1987 and lived together in Thailand for several years before returning to the States for good in 1993.

Luckily, during his extensive research John was able to locate a very early recording of Marty reading the codex, including the lost thirteenth page. It is a very important page because it culminates with the New Fire ceremony, a finale to the initiatory spiritual journey encoded into in the codex. The reinstatement of the thirteenth page occurred in the summer of 2000, while Marty was living his final days in Brooklyn, the town of his birth. He was just delighted that John was able to transcribe the final page from such a poor recording, and with that, was content that the codex was completely restored and ready to be tossed into the winds of posterity.

As John suggests in chapter 1, the Pyramid of Fire should be called officially the Codex Matz-Ayauhtla, and deservedly so. Marty devoted an extreme amount of effort to receiving and preserving its sacred pages, and he refused all criticism from anthropologists, archaeologists, scholars, and anyone else who had discouraging words for his work. He was determined

---

* Both this and the epigraph are from "A Funny Thing Happened on My Way to Enlightenment" by Martin Matz, *In the Seasons of My Eye* (New York: Panther Books, 2004).

that the value of the codex be understood and recognized for its profound knowledge and emphasized time and again that realizations on many levels will come to those who study it. He never gave up.

As this book is now in your hands, I hope that you too will study it until some special realizations sink in, for they surely will. In giving this brief background it is my humble hope to offer a personal glimpse of Marty that will enrich your enjoyment and appreciation of the knowledge contained herein.

I dedicate this book in loving memory of Marty and with deepest gratitude to John Major Jenkins for his commitment to bringing this book to fruition and presenting it to the public.

BARBARA A. MATZ

Preface:
A Note on the Contents

The somewhat unusual structure of this book has been conceived to allow for incorporating Marty Matz's unpublished writings relating to the Aztec codex called the Pyramid of Fire.

In 1995 Marty and I began working together on a book about this previously unknown codex, and the introduction he wrote for that text appears here. In it he emphasizes that the Pyramid of Fire belongs to the perennial tradition—that is, the wisdom it contains is universal and eternal.

Following the introduction, in chapter 1 readers will find both a brief biography of Marty Matz and a discussion of the codex's authenticity and origin.

Chapter 2 consists of an autobiographical short story by Marty, "In Search of Paititi," in which he recounts his arrival and early adventures in Mexico in the late 1950s up to the time just before he finds the village of the codex, where his search for Paititi ends. Paititi, sought by seekers from time immemorial, is the legendary paradise city that ends the spiritual quest.

Chapter 3 comprises an unfinished novella by Marty structured upon all thirteen pages of the Pyramid of Fire. It reads much like an initiatory experience, and though it is incomplete, we can determine the general contents of its final chapter by extrapolating from the events detailed on the thirteenth (and final) page of the codex. All of Marty's writings found here, including the poem "Time Waits" (see page vi), supply clues to help us better understand the nature of the codex as well as his interpretation of it.

Following the novella, the text of the codex itself appears in chapter 4, with standardized pages and line numbers.

In 1995 I produced a detailed explication of and commentary on the first five pages of the codex, identifying some embedded cosmological points of interest that Marty himself was unaware of (a good indication that he did not create the codex). My own evolving understanding of and experience with the Pyramid of Fire derives from working with it as a profound initiatory text and guidebook rather than from studying it objectively from an academic perspective. In chapter 5 I share a three-part commentary on the codex, consisting of a page-by-page exegesis, a summary of Marty's own observations, and a dialogue between Marty and me that conveys a glimpse of our relationship. Some of Marty's comments are so succinct that I have transcribed them directly, while I have taken this opportunity to expand upon others, such as those relating to astronomy and certain teachings of mystic philosopher G. I. Gurdjieff.

As for tackling the codex itself, I can testify that reading it aloud helps in understanding its deeper meanings and that learning to pronounce the often tongue-twisting names of the Nahuatl deities is essential to feeling their mantric power. (To this end, a brief pronunciation guide precedes chapter 4 and phonetic pronunciations of all Nahuatl deities in the codex are given in appendix 2.)

To develop a relationship with the Pyramid of Fire is to develop a relationship with the perennial philosophy. While I hope to convey some of what I have gleaned from it, most important is that the text is now available for all to read and study according to their own lights—guided, it is hoped, by the mystic spirit of the Nahuatl *tlamatinime*, the poet-philosophers.

Finally, and importantly, chapter 6 compares the Pyramid of Fire to other examples of visionary ascent literature—most notably Hebrew Scripture and Gnostic sources—and compares its concepts to those of Taoism and Hinduism. The interwoven themes in this chapter include that of the *ekpyrosis* (universal conflagration at the end of an age), death as an ascent, apocalypse imagery, tantric sublimation yoga, the culmination of the New Fire tradition as a precession-based World Age doctrine, and personal sacrifice as a necessary precursor to spiritual growth. The very fact that these universal themes are expressed in an Aztec codex is significant and supports Marty's assertion (pioneered by Nahuatl translator Miguel León-Portilla) that Aztec religion belongs to the perennial philosophy.

As I explain in chapter 6, the presence of Gnostic elements does not mean that Nahuatl religion was body- and world-denying (a common criticism of Gnosticism) but instead that it regarded all things on earth as impermanent, transitory, and subject to the laws of birth, growth, and death. In this view a great truth of Buddhist teachings is found in the codex, that of *impermanence*—the only constant is change. Like the Zen philosophers of Asia, the Nahuatl poet-philosophers (the *tlamatinime*) searched for and found a higher source and ground of being that, like the perennial wisdom itself, is undying.

Nahuatl Poetry
and Metaphysics

In Vedanta and Hebrew prophecy, in the Tao Teh King and the
Platonic dialogues, in the Gospel according to St. John and
Mahayana theology, in Plotinus and the Areopagite, among the
Persian Sufis and the Christian Mystics of the Middle Ages and
the Renaissance—the Perennial Philosophy has spoken almost all
the languages of Asia and Europe and has made use of the
terminology and traditions of every one of the higher religions.
But under all this confusion of tongues and myths, of local
histories and particularist doctrines, there remains the Highest
Common Factor, which is the Perennial Philosophy in what may
be called its chemically pure state.

ALDOUS HUXLEY, INTRODUCTION TO
THE SONG OF GOD, BHAGAVAD-GITA

The following introduction was written by Martin Matz in Healdsburg,
California, in September 1997.

The Pyramid of Fire is a previously unknown Aztec codex (hieroglyphic
manuscript) which was most probably painted in the last half of the fifteenth century. The content of Aztec codices was very likely more varied
than the existing examples seem to indicate, with the great majority being

ritualistic and divinatory. The Pyramid of Fire belongs to this group of divinatory works, which were called in Nahuatl (the language of the Aztecs) *tonalamatl* or *tonalpohualli,* "the book of the days." These books were all calendars consisting of 260 days, a number that was arrived at by sequentially combining twenty day signs with thirteen numbers. The tonalpohualli guidebook was used to determine whether a day would be fortunate or unfortunate. We will return to this subject in greater detail in chapter 3.

The Pyramid of Fire, however, is much more than just a divinatory calendar. It is an American version of the perennial philosophy that can be compared to the Kabbalah, alchemy, Western astrology, Hermetic philosophy, the teachings of Gurdjieff, and the tarot in order to show that all occult knowledge stems from a single source. Because Asia and Europe are a contiguous landmass, no one disputes the idea that by means of travel, trade, and conquest the great civilizations of the ancient and classical world influenced each other. Therefore, it is not so surprising to find the perennial philosophy expressed in various forms even in such geographically distant locations as China, India, Egypt, the Middle East, Greece, and Rome.

The situation in the Americas was supposedly entirely different. Archaeologists have steadfastly insisted that each of the high cultures and great civilizations of the New World developed independently—that is to say, without contact or influence from outside people. This completely erroneous theory of independent development has been taught as absolute truth throughout the twentieth century.

Before proceeding with the text of the codex, I would like to offer some background on the philosophy and metaphysical concepts of the Aztecs.

The codices were mnemonic devices (memory aids) for recording all the sciences and wisdom of which the Aztecs had knowledge. The *tlamatinime* (knowers of things) were wise men, those initiated into occult knowledge, and were responsible for composing, painting books, and knowing and teaching the songs and poems in which were preserved the Aztec sciences, wisdom, and mysteries. The Aztecs found in the rhythm of poetry an easy and accurate way of remembering the meaning of the hieroglyphs inscribed in their manuscripts.

It is impossible to overemphasize the importance of poetry in shaping the forms and thoughts expressed by the high cultures and great civilizations of ancient America. Without knowledge of what the Aztecs called "flower and song" (poetry), we can neither understand nor appreciate the true greatness of their achievements. Only the Mexican scholar and Nahuatl translator Miguel León-Portilla has seriously studied this subject and written about it. I feel indebted to him and wish to express my deep gratitude for his pioneering work.[1]

The perennial philosophy has appeared and reappeared in various guises and been expressed in numberless ways throughout the ages. Nowhere, however, has the secret knowledge been presented in so aesthetically pleasing a manner or reached so high an artistic level as it has in the Pyramid of Fire. The power of the poetry used to express the perennial philosophy in the codex makes this work unique in the realm of occult literature.

The tlamatinime recognized as clearly as most ancient philosophers and wise men the transitory nature of earthly things. The great Aztec king Nezahualcoyotl of Texcoco captures this quality of evanescence in the following lines:

> *Is it true that on earth one lives?*
> *Not forever on earth, only a little while.*
> *Though jade it may be, it breaks;*
> *though gold it may be, it is crushed;*
> *though it be quetzal plumes, it shall not last.*
> *Not forever on earth, only a little while.*[2]

If everything is transitory, if the world in which we live is fated to end in cataclysm, as preceding ages have done, then it is inevitable that we ask ourselves if life is a kind of unreal dream, if we can be certain of knowing anything. In the last quarter of the fifteenth century this search for answers led to a gathering of wise men in the house of Tecoyehuatzin, king of Huexotzinco. The purpose of this meeting, given in their own words, was to discuss the meaning of poetry, flower, and song in the deepest sense. The opinions of those present were diverse. For some, "flower and song" provided a means for drawing closer to the deity; for others it signified only that which makes friendship and understanding possible among human beings. For King Ayocuan, poetry was the only thing of value that man could leave behind on earth as a remembrance. For other tlamatinime, it was the best creative outlet for consoling princes and wise men.

Finally, King Tecoyehuatzin offered his perspective. He saw poetry as the only means of speaking words that can bring the truth to humans in a world that is like a dream, a world in which everything is transitory and that, like a quetzal feather, ultimately falls apart. These are King Tecoyehuatzin's words:

> Now do I hear the words of the coyolli bird
> as he makes answer to the Giver of Life.
> He goes his way singing, offering flowers.
> And his words rain down
> like jade and quetzal plumes.
> Is that what pleases the Giver of Life?
> Is that the only truth on earth?[3]

In spite of the universal evanescence of existence, the tlamatinime concluded that there is a way to know the truth and that way is poetry, for which "flower and song" is both symbol and metaphor. Juan García Bacca noted in his comments on Martin Heidegger's *Holderlin and the Essence of Poetry*: "*meta*-phor and *meta*-physics have basically and fundamentally one and the same function: to put things 'beyond.'"[4] Thus, poetry, as a vehicle of metaphysical expression relying on metaphors, is an attempt to vitiate the transitory nature of earthly things. The wise men of Mexico did not believe they could form rational images of what is beyond, but they were convinced that through metaphors, by means of poetry, truth was attainable. This attitude was rooted in their belief in the divine origin of poetry, that it comes from above. Poetry intoxicates, enraptures, and by intensifying the emotions and the perceptual powers, it enables the poet to perceive what would ordinarily be undetectable. Real or authentic poetry is born of inspiration emanating from beyond—

from what is above. And it is this inspiration that enables man to speak the only truth on earth. In referring to the Aztecs and other Meso-americans, the French archaeologist Jacques Soustelle hit the nail on the head when he wrote that theirs was one of the few cultures of which "mankind can be proud."[5]

Given that the Pyramid of Fire, like other central Mexican hiero-glyphic books, was intended to be a device for recalling the poetry and song that conveyed the truths of Aztec cosmology, the fact that a Mazatec shaman read me its contents makes this codex unique. It is like a book with a voice in a field of other books containing mute pictures. There are many such surviving Nahuatl books, and scholars have attempted to reconstruct the content of each based upon their own interpretations and efforts. Confusions, conceptual biases, and erroneous assumptions can be expected with this approach. The Pyramid of Fire, however, comes straight from the mouth, so to speak, and therefore provides an unam-biguous window into the ancient Aztec mind and a record of the peren-nial philosophy as it manifested among the ancient Aztecs. It is the long-awaited key to unlocking the secrets of Aztec philosophy, calendar sci-ence, and mythology.

Marty Matz and the Lost Codex

It is a fallacia consequentis *to equate a polyglot with a translator, a scholar with a writer. Apart from the mere circumstance that they all deal with words, there is no necessity to suppose they have anything in common. Translations must have poets at both ends of the process.*

JOHN GREENWAY,
A HISTORY OF ANCIENT MEXICO

Marty Matz: The Mystic Nomad Forever Moving

Martin Matz was born in Brooklyn in 1934 and grew up in an Italian and Jewish neighborhood in Bensonhurst. His father died when he was ten years old, and he relocated with his mother to Omaha, Nebraska, when she remarried a short time later. Marty said in an interview in *Goodie Magazine*: "I hated it. Oh boy, man, terrible. The wasteland of all the world. You know, I come from New York. My father used to take me to museums and concerts and art galleries, and in Nebraska there wasn't anything like that."[1]

Marty survived his high school years in the Midwest, graduating as a wrestling champion, and then studied art for a year at the nearby University of Nebraska. When the Korean War needed recruits, he volunteered to be an Army Reserve alpine ski instructor (even though he'd never been on skis) and trained in Colorado. During this time a car accident left him with a neck broken in three places and a broken back. While laid up in an army hospital for a year, he picked up his liking for drugs.

After being discharged fate found him in New York City, hanging out in Greenwich Village and ingratiating himself with those in the emerging Beat scene. At this time Marty started writing poetry. It was 1955, before Jack Kerouac published *On the Road* and before Allen Ginsberg published *Howl.* Ironically, Marty didn't meet any of these incipient Beat luminaries until he crossed the country in 1956 and landed in San Francisco. Along the way, in Amarillo, Texas, he gave a poetry reading accompanied by Dizzie Gillespie—probably one of the first jazz-poetry performances that eventually came to define Beat poetics. (The "Bird" in the poem excerpt below refers to jazz musician Charlie "Bird" Parker.)

On his first day in San Francisco he met local poet Bob Kaufman. Together they found rooms at the Swiss American Hotel and wrote poetry deep into the night. Soon after, for $35 a month they rented a seven-room railroad flat, which became a kind of West Coast annex of the Village.

The kings of the Beats came and went—Jack Kerouac, Neal Cassady, Gregory Corso, Allen Ginsberg. Marty became particularly close to Corso and Bob Kaufman. Years later, he would be "a thoughtful and comforting presence" during Corso's final months battling cancer, and his words were "among the most moving at the memorial service for Corso."[2] Marty often dedicated poems to his close friends, and his poem for Bob Kaufman, entitled "I Know Where Rainbows Go to Die," has been called a "poignant, original, and beautiful tribute that has to be one of the great poems of our time."[3] It reads in part:

> *Together we walked through a fabled city*
> *of hallucinating green*
> *And talked away*
> *a thousand smoking nights*
> *As your aching heart*
> *beat its bones*
> *in time to Bird's brilliant sounds*
> *over the neon streets of murdered schemes*[4]

Marty is the unknown Beat poet who followed the beat of a different drum even within the progressive milieu of the late-1950s Beat scene itself. Just a few months before Ginsberg's *Howl* was published and called attention to the doings of all his cronies and colleagues, Marty went south to Mexico, and over the next twenty-one years he returned to the Bay Area only for brief visits. We can catch a glimpse of his Mexican adventures in his short story "In Search of Paititi" (see chapter 2) and can also refer to stories he told to friends and interviewers.

In 1957 he first went to Yalapa, near Puerto Vallarta on the west coast of Mexico. At that time this little village was still a remote enclave of artists and pot-smoking rebels; it took days to get there from Mexico City, though today it is a popular tourist resort. Marty and his friends rented a stone house in Yalapa for the equivalent of $4 a month. On a visit to nearby Puerto Vallarta he met film director John Huston and invited him out to the house. For three days straight they told stories, drank, and got high. Before long, with a letter of recommendation from Huston, Marty was taking some classes in anthropology and pre-Columbian art in Guadalajara. He worked for Huston for about a year, collecting pre-Columbian antiquities, which required long forays into remote mountain areas in the states of Guerrero and Oaxaca. Such activity was dangerous, involving making deals with shady local officials and hiring local peasants to dig into mounds in search of artifacts. It was also ethically dubious and Marty knew it, but he found it amusingly ironic that several well-known academic scholars from the United States hired him to locate objects. Marty's fame as an independent antiquities expert grew to the extent that he was used as a consultant for an article appearing in *National Geographic*.

During his wanderings in the state of Oaxaca, Marty made frequent trips into Mazatec country. By 1960 he was busy compiling a five-hundred-word Mazatec language dictionary and had become quite close to the Mazatec shaman who eventually showed him the codex that would become the Pyramid of Fire. Recognizing the importance of such a find, Marty returned briefly to the Bay Area in 1961, where he fine-tuned the translation of the codex and performed it in poetry clubs. It is at this time that he and Kerouac were recorded reading their poetry, and Marty's early reading of the codex has survived.

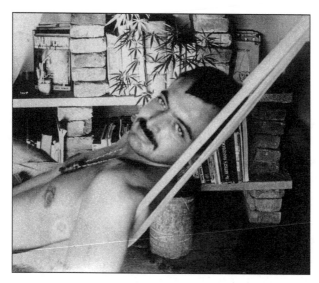

Fig. 1.1. Marty Matz in Mexico, circa 1960

In the early 1960s Marty married a Mexican woman, and when her father died, they ran his ice factory together in the state of Veracruz. While Marty was away collecting pre-Columbian art, tragedy struck: his wife was killed in an accident at the factory. They had been married almost nine years.

Eventually Marty expanded his wanderings from Mexico to South America. Always seeking the least trodden path, he passed the years in long marijuana-drenched poetry idylls, drug dealing, and art collecting. Once he was bitten by a snake in Mexico while crossing a river, and though his lower leg turned an ugly purple, he kept going. In one of his own poems he characterizes himself as "forever moving":

> *I am the perpetual wanderer*
> *the insatiable traveler*
> *the mystic nomad*
> *forever moving*
> *towards some strange horizon*
> *of twisted dimensions*
> *and chaotic dreams.*[5]

On another occasion he was stricken by a flesh-eating parasite, and doctors told him that they would need to amputate his infected arm. Ignoring them, he instead found a shaman who for two weeks administered preparations of the potent visionary and psychoactive vine known as ayahuasca and cured him by "throwing light" into the darkness.[6]

Marty was brilliant and resourceful in many ways. His friends tell of a five-step extraction process he developed to dissolve cocaine into a liquid form that could be dried onto souvenir plates and shipped to the United States, where the white powder was reclaimed by reversing the process. Stories are legion of Marty hosting great parties, renting lavish properties for months at a time, and buying property in various locations. But all the while, the poetry kept flowing. In the wild fortunes of such living, the money that is made is largely an inconsequential side benefit; Marty squandered it as soon as it appeared. His drug dealing eventually got him into trouble, but before it did, he was in serious danger of becoming rich.

The roaming of the "insatiable wanderer" was brought to a halt when Marty was arrested in Mexico in 1974 for possession of a small amount of cocaine and grass. Thus a new chapter in his adventurous life was launched, one that he reveled in recounting but that often evokes cringing tears from those who hear it. He spent almost four years in Mexico's infamous Lecumberi prison, a corrupt, dingy, horrendously violent place where, during his first months of incarceration, he saw fifty-seven people killed. In Lecumberi everything, including survival, had to be bargained and bribed for on a daily basis. In a detailed interview in *Goodie Magazine*, Marty recounts many aborted escape attempts, including the end game that almost cost him his life: After hiding in a tunnel for three days, he and an accomplice were discovered and almost shot, but were saved at the last moment by a fluke of fate. As they were being escorted by their captors to certain doom, reporters arrived for a tour of the prison. In order to avoid a media fiasco, Marty and his accomplice were spirited away to relative safety.

After the Lecumberi prison was shut down, Marty served another year in Santa Marta prison—certainly no rose garden—until finally, in 1978, he succeeded in winning release in an amnesty program. According to his wife, filmmaker Barbara Matz, whom Marty wed in the late 1980s, the fortlike Lecumberi prison has since been renovated to hold the Mexican government's national archives. Cells that once held prisoners now contain shelves loaded with books, files, and documents. Once known as the Palacio Negro, a repository of the living dead, Lecumberi is now a repository of information.

After his release from prison Marty returned to San Francisco, renewing old friendships and continuing to write, read, and organize his poetry. He traveled several times to New York City and haunted the old poetry dens of the Village. His book *Time Waits: Selected Poems 1956–1986* was published in 1987 (JMF Publishing; revised and expanded in 1994). He and Barbara periodically held convivial poetry salons in rooms at the Chelsea Hotel in Manhattan.

In 1988, when Marty and Barbara were invited to attend the Tenth World Congress of Poets in Bangkok, Thailand, they decided to go six months early to tour the country at a casual traveler's pace. After only three days in Bangkok, Marty was hit by a truck while crossing a street and broke his collarbone. He was hospitalized briefly, after which the couple caught a train as soon as they could to the town of Chiang Mai, near the poppy fields of northern Thailand. Upon hearing there of the Lahu hill tribe to the north, they ventured by truck into the Golden Triangle, where they stayed in a bamboo hut for a very nominal sum. They walked the final six mountainous miles to the remote Lahu village, briefly stopping only to cook a few pipes full of opium. They stayed in the village until the World Congress of Poets began and afterward returned to the Lahu hills with an entourage of poets in tow.

There they lingered for several years, living off Barbara's inheritance in a languid and lavish opium-filled lifestyle. During this time Marty's beautiful Oriental visions were immortalized in his poetry collection *Pipe Dreams*, designed and published by Barbara in 1991 and including an introduction by his friend and Beat storyteller Herbert Huncke.

Marty and Barbara also traveled in China, Burma, Hong Kong, Laos, Cambodia, Malaysia, Vietnam, and India to buy tribal art and antiquities while enjoying the scenery. By 1993 the money was running out, which led them to relocate to northern California, where

Marty again began trying to interest people in the Pyramid of Fire.

In 1994, having been given my phone number by writer and explorer Terence McKenna, Marty contacted me and told me about the Aztec codex he'd received. At first I was skeptical: an *unknown* Aztec codex? Oh, not the original, he asserted, just a transcription of one. My doubts continued: The drawings of the original pictographs were now lost? . . . Who was Marty Matz, after all? He was an expatriot Beat poet who had danced with Allen Ginsberg, read poetry with Jack Kerouac, and spent most of the past thirty-seven years living in Third World countries—and now he was back in the States, seeking to interest scholars and poets in the Pyramid of Fire.

I soon realized that Marty's codex was indeed a rare and valuable contribution to understanding Nahuatl cosmology and metaphysics. Together we worked up an outline for a proposed book, which included Marty's introduction (see pages 1–5). I recorded phone interviews with him in late 1995 and submitted the book proposal to several publishers, but as it happened, none were interested.

As 1997 wore on the insatiable wanderer once again heard the call. Marty left again for Mexico. We exchanged letters while he was living in Oaxaca in 1998, then he disappeared. Two years later he contacted me again. He had come full circle and was back in Brooklyn with good news to share: He had found a warm following for his poetry in Italy after joining a group of poets including Ira Cohen, Lawrence Ferlinghetti, and Anne Waldman. He had stayed with friends in Rome for a year, where he enjoyed praise and recognition for his poetic gifts. His wife, Barbara, joined him there for the 1999–2000 Millennium Ceremony. Marty was calling to ask me to set up an official Web site for him and to reissue *Pipe Dreams,* which now included his recent poem "The Alchemist's Song" and an introduction by Peter Lee. By November 2000 I had completed this task, redesigning both the book's cover and interior.[7]

In his city of birth at the turn of the millennium Marty was busy recording with Church of Betty, an avant-garde musical group led by sitar player Chris Rael. In the last summer of his life he made two important recordings: a CD entitled "A Sky of Fractured Feathers" and a soon-to-be-released complete reading of *Pipe Dreams.*[8] Marty and Church of

Betty also performed live together at the Brooklyn Museum of Art and the Gershwin Hotel, with Marty reading his poetry. I sent him $20 bills and spoke with him on the phone often during the winter of 2000–2001. We talked about life, liberty, and the pursuit of poetry.

One problem with Marty's translation of the codex, I noticed from my copy, was that the thirteenth page was missing. So he had his friend Bobby Yarra send me an old recording of Marty himself reading the Pyramid of Fire, from which I was able to recover and transcribe the missing thirteenth page. At the time I was deeply mired in commuting fifty-five miles a day to an unfulfilling dot-com position, and Marty's oft-repeated advice was to "quit that fuckin' job!" By May of 2001 I was a free man, and in June, due to a car snafu, I just barely missed seeing him read at the Spaghetti Factory in New York City.

Marty had often mentioned his increasing physical distress and difficulty walking. By then (mid-2001) he weighed more than three hundred pounds. He had made a difficult journey west to visit with his dying friend Gregory Corso, who called Marty "my Matzoh Ball." In Marty's final months in an apartment on the Lower East Side, he received old friends and a new generation of admirers while watching the San Francisco 49ers and the Yankee playoffs. He told a friend that he regretted nothing and bragged with characteristic humor that he "was the laziest man in the world—and getting better at it every day," a statement that captures his self-effacing humor but detracts from the truth: he was a master word weaver, a luminous though overshadowed voice in Beat poetics, and an instrumental force in the recovery and elucidation of a lost document of Nahuatl cosmological poetry.

Marty died just after sundown on October 28, 2001.

The Authenticity of the Codex

Marty's devotion to being a wandering bhiku-bum poet was the preeminent guiding force of his life—and who is to say that this is detrimental to finding truth? The boon-bestowing goddess opens spiritual secrets to the seeker who is unfettered by the chains of worldly ambition. For Marty, finding the Pyramid of Fire was the answer to his search for

Paititi. This much shines through in his writings. But our suspicions about this codex may still linger; in the end, how do we know the Pyramid of Fire is an authentic text and not just a poetic fantasy?

The question may simply be impossible to answer conclusively. However, an objective assessment of several factors might help to solidify the case for its authenticity. As I have mentioned, I myself was suspicious at first but was convinced by two sets of information: the consistencies encoded within the codex itself—a patterning beyond the conscious machinations of anyone perpetrating a hoax—and Marty's behavior and responses when I confronted him with my doubts.

Marty testified that he himself could not have created the codex, and his friends and wife concur. In fact, in surveying the style of his writings, we find many very beautiful and striking visionary poems, but nothing with the cosmological intricacy of the Pyramid of Fire.

In addition, some of the themes I was able to reconstruct in my initial commentary on the first five pages of the codex took Marty by surprise. In order to have created the text himself, he would have to have been a poet, cosmologist, and a clever encryption artist.

In two volumes of *The Handbook of Middle American Indians* we find detailed studies of central Mexican codices and a reference to an ancient picture book from Ayauhtla, reportedly viewed there in the 1700s but now missing.[9] Initially, I believed that this could indeed be the codex Marty had transcribed. When I pointed this out to him, however, he did not jump to embrace the potential evidence, as a huckster who had fabricated the codex might have done. Instead, he highly doubted my suggestion because of the extremely reticent nature of the Ayauhtla Mazatecs and don Daniel's family mission of guardianship over the codex. According to don Daniel, the Pyramid of Fire had remained hidden since the Conquest. Marty surmised that the "lost" *lienzo* (painted canvas) referred to was probably a native history that, like so many others, had been taken out of hiding to be shown or copied but eventually decayed beyond salvation or was itself lost.

To this evidence of the authenticity of the codex is added the text's content, the depth of which suggests that Marty could not have created it. Certainly it's reasonable to suspect that some potentially important features do get lost in the process of transcribing and translating an original pictographic document. But if we study the Pyramid of Fire and explore its inner meanings, we find deep esoteric ideas and principles that Marty would have been hard pressed to produce on his own.

Yet of course he left his mark on the Pyramid of Fire. The echoes of his verbiage, which we can hear at certain spots in the codex, are undeniably his imprint as translator of the Mazatec and Spanish. While he may have taken both poetic license in labeling deities that are difficult to identify and liberties in fleshing out the mathematics on page 5, and while he might have added a few lines of contextual segue, none of this means the codex itself is his work. Elias Lönnrot, the great compiler of backwoods oral tradition that became the Finnish national epic, the *Kalevala*, was once accused of largely devising it himself. Careful examination, however, showed that of the 22,850 verses of the *Kalevala* only a very small amount were attributable to Lönnrot, and most of those were irrelevant transitions between chapters.[10]

Marty was trusted with the responsibility of translating the codex and preserving its inner meaning. In translating any text we run the risk of generating ambiguities or even errors. Once I realized how profoundly the contents of the codex spoke for its own authenticity, I felt no need to cross-examine Marty relentlessly on how he undertook the transcription and translation process. I have always had the sense that he resisted adding his own elaborations to the text. Questions may remain about how much he improvised or added while making the English translation of the codex, but at some point we simply must trust that Marty did his best and was as faithful as humanly possible to the teaching that was read to him.

Marty himself was a shaman of sorts, a visionary poet who could see and understand the deep metaphysical teachings within the Pyramid of Fire and transmit them to others. Due to the modern world's uncanny knack for ignoring authentic information and celebrating sensationalized falsehood, the task of transmitting is very often thankless and disappointing—evidenced by the fact that it has taken more than forty years for the translation to finally come into print while blatant fantasy/allegory books easily skyrocket to the top of the bestseller lists. Granted, suspicions about the text's authenticity may have been at the root of Marty's decades-long fruitless quest for publication of the codex, but it is unfortunate that no one was intrigued enough to take the time to carefully assess what he was trying to share. Perhaps because there was no treasure trove of gold artifacts involved the pursuit was deemed not worthwhile. Yet the real treasures in the Pyramid of Fire are not external riches but inner gnosis—a gnosis that cannot be reached without personal sacrifice. The relationship between personal sacrifice and the experience of gnosis, or divine wisdom, is a central teaching of the Pyramid of Fire that will be explored more deeply in later chapters.

There exists a recording of the Pyramid of Fire made by Marty and Jack Kerouac on a wire recorder in the early 1960s. From it we can conclude that the text was completed by then, but it has been difficult to pin down the precise time the codex was shown to Marty. He himself said he received it over several sessions in 1961. In the phone conversations I recorded with Marty in 1995 and 1996, the details he supplied about his time in Mexico make it plausible that the Pyramid of Fire was read to him in early 1961. He told me that he studied and drew sketches of the pictures from the codex that was shown to him on several occasions, and he was later able to identify similar images in Aztec codices that were already known. Marty copied some of these images and placed them alongside the text of the Pyramid of Fire that he sent to me. I've located other relevant pictures based on Marty's direction and from my own comparative study of the known codices.

When he returned to the States briefly in 1961, Marty carefully identified the correct spellings of the various deities mentioned in the Pyramid of Fire, mainly using León-Portilla's in-depth study of central Mexican mythology.[11] We also know that Marty performed the text in the San Francisco poetry scene of the early 1960s, as well as in the late 1970s.

In the introduction to this book (see page 1), Marty notes three important themes found in or relating to the codex: the Nahuatl appreciation of the concept of impermanence, the Nahuatl understanding of the spiritually transforming power of poetry and song, and the codex itself existing as a rare artifact of contemporary Native dramaturgy (dramatic performance of religious teachings). The first theme—the Nahuatl appreciation for the philosophical concept of impermanence—will be treated in more detail in chapter 6. The second theme, that of the power of poetry and song to transport the poet—and the audience—into an altered, spiritual state in which hidden realities are perceived, is something Marty could appreciate as a poet and is a defining characteristic of Nahuatl poetry and metaphysics. Such a perspective emphasizes that sacred texts like the Pyramid of Fire must be performed (or read aloud) in order to evoke a true understanding, or gnostic/inner transmutation, of their contents.

Finally, the third theme that Marty notes—the unique value of the Pyramid of Fire as a text that was read and interpreted by an authentic holder of its lineage—deserves a bit of explanation. The village shaman named don Daniel was descended from a family of Mazatec nobility, adjuncts to the Aztec throne at the time of the Conquest. After the Conquest Franciscan missionaries, such as Bernardino de Sahagún, desired to learn more about their conquered subjects. Likewise, the Central Mexican people, including the surviving Aztecs, Mazatecs, Mixtecs, and other Nahuatl (central Mexican) groups, wished to preserve their sciences and histories and began producing picture books after the pre-Conquest style.

Some of these books, now in museums, were appropriated by the Spanish and were in fact created before the Conquest. Some were simple maps of villages, showing trade relations with neighboring communities. Some were pictographic histories of recent battles and events. Many, however, were filled with complicated cosmogonic diagrams, creation myths, and calendar charts and contained spiritual lessons for those human beings who wished to be initiated into the eternal mysteries of life and death. The codices referred to as Nuttall, Borgia, and Borbonicus are perhaps the best known in this category. They come down to us today as mute sentinels of a grand cosmic vision that, in lieu of an informed interpreter, are endlessly puzzled over by scholars and experts. There are academic commentaries and analyses, of course, but they are after the fashion of analytical guesswork and lack the depth a native teacher might bring to the interpretation of these texts.

In eastern Mesoamerica, where the Maya live, surviving hieroglyphic books are even more rare than the picture books of central Mexico. In fact, there are only four surviving Mayan books—the Paris, Dresden,

Madrid, and Grolier codices. It is believed, however, that the Popol Vuh, the great creation myth of the Quiché Maya, was rendered into alphabetic script by a group of Quiché elders reading directly from a hieroglyphic book in the 1550s.[12] That book was never found, though it may still be held in secret or may be buried somewhere in the environs of Chichicastenango, Guatemala. The hieroglyphic books, like the central Mexican picture books, were memory devices that enabled initiated lineage keepers or teachers to "perform" the contents of the book for an audience or for selected initiates. Thus, the text of the Quiché Popol Vuh, now translated into many languages, is unique in that it represents one of the only known examples of a native picture book read, interpreted, and transcribed by members of an authentic teaching lineage. This is very significant; because it is an initiatory text, much would be lost if only the pictures remained and there was no key to its interpretation.

The Pyramid of Fire can now be placed alongside the Popol Vuh as a rare example of a native picture book interpreted by an authentic native teacher. As with the Popol Vuh, we do not have the original text of the Pyramid of Fire. But more important, we have a transcription of it that was "performed" with the "key" of initiatory knowledge. Marty's role in bringing forth the Pyramid of Fire was twofold: First, after years of friendship, don Daniel chose him to be the one to share the knowledge with the outer world. Second, Marty's skill as a poet and speaker of Mazatec, English, and Spanish allowed him to faithfully render the text into an English version that beautifully preserves hidden meanings, which we can reconstruct through careful study. Out of respect for the reticence of the Ayauhtla Mazatecs and to preserve their land from anything resembling the 1960s hippie invasion of nearby Huatla de Jimenez, travel to Ayauhtla in the pursuit of finding the codex is strongly discouraged. Marty believed it was still there, but it would be virtually impossible for any outsider to win the confidence required to see it. In addition, a contact of mine who lives in Huatla has himself—because he is an outsider—been the subject of what can politely be called "Mazatec witchcraft." He advises that shamanic witchcraft is serious business, and the Mazatecs of Ayauhtla are notorious for protecting their secrets. In order for the Mazatecs to reveal the codex to him, it took Marty years of friendship building, not a little personal sacrifice, the enduring of initiations, and the gift of a special providence known only to the Aztec deities. A very ancient adage is appropriate here: Treasure hunters should beware the dangers of seeking external riches and instead turn inward for the real gold.

Cerro Rabon is a sacred cave-riddled mountain not far from Ayauhtla. It has been visited by many spelunkers and might be a good destination for adventurous souls wishing to enter the environs where the codex was found. Strange mysteries orbit Cerro Rabon, as is suggested by its use in J. J. Hurtak's *The Keys of Enoch* and in some interpretations of the Book of Mormon.* It should also be mentioned that the cave in Cerro Rabon that is featured in the novella *The Pyramid of Fire* (see chapter 3) is a place where Marty has said he was brought for ceremonies, although it might not actually appear as he describes it in the story.

To honor Marty's indispensable role in bringing the codex to light, and in recognition of where it comes from and the fact that Marty was chosen by the codex's keeper as the one to present it to the world, I propose the codex be officially called the Codex Matz-Ayauhtla. Informally we may still refer to it as the Pyramid of Fire.

---

* Such visits might be planned in the future. Those interested in further information may contact me at John@alignment2012.com.

2 In Search of Paititi

When the dust of Mexico covers the intestines of my dreams, I shall return. When maguey spines burn the wind and the skulls of dogs pierce the dawn, I will be there. Broken bottles and crooked graves disturb the adobe sky. Indians dressed in the horns of icicles dance on the roots of July. Mexico—the smell of rancid grease and sunlight sticks to the armpits of my tortured serape. Mexico—the stones of Palenque transfix my navel. Mexico! And I am lost in a liquorish afternoon, stuck to the sun's side where barrels of moss sing in the ruins of ancient dreams. This is the way it was, is, shall always be, with one foot stuck in a pool of burning mirrors and the other spinning a frenzy of microscopes as clocks rape the frozen ash of rivers and turn hummingbirds to brass on a mountain covered with teeth.*

Call me John X or, if you prefer, Mr. Anonymous. Who I am is not important, but the story is. I first went to Mexico in 1957. At the time I didn't realize that when I crossed the border, I also passed to the other side of Alice's looking glass, into a place far stranger than any Wonderland.

The Pan-American Highway that would eventually run from the U.S. border all the way to Tierra del Fuego at the southern tip of South America was then a two-lane road that ended on the outskirts of the Federal District, Mexico City. It took a professional optimist with a vivid

---

* This paragraph is a modified prose version of Marty's poem "When Maguey Spines Burn the Wind," from *Time Waits: Selected Poems 1956–1986* (San Francisco: JMF Publishing, 1987). Barbara Matz Alexander reports that Marty's original intention was to make "In Search of Paititi" a novel, beginning each chapter with one of his poems, but later he considered it a short story. He seemed to have taken up the idea of a novel with his writing of the first three chapters of the novella *The Pyramid of Fire* (see chapter 3). —*JMJ*

imagination to call that road a highway. Stretching hundreds upon hundreds of miles, it was paved in short sections that were separated by long bone-rattling expanses of deep mud.

Most people see Mexico as a place or a nation or a geographical location that can be pinpointed on a map. For me, Mexico is a transcendental space, a magical enchanted Kingdom of Oz or a surrealistic circus. The manifest reality of everyday Mexican life in any other place on earth would be viewed as preposterous, absurd, and definitely impossible.

At some point during my early years of wandering Mexico, the Pan-American Highway turned into a psychedelic green-cactus road and I learned to look for the things that were not there in order to see what was. I sought for a secret existence that I felt through the pores of my skin. I learned to recognize the fragility of a situation and in that instant of recognition convert it without emphasis into a fatal alternative, a decisive manifestation. I thought of destinies, not acts, and thereby decided without sentimentality the course of my life.

Listen friends, if you live in Mexico for long stretches of time, it can make you wise or it can kill you, but I can guarantee that whatever happens, it will never be the thing you expected. Over the years my feelings about Mexico shifted from love to hatred and back to love. Once, when I was living in Mexico City, I woke in the morning with the overpowering urge to fly away from all danger, but I was capable only of attempting a ludicrous shuffle while stumbling through the exotic flowers that grew on the top of a hard Mexican wall, unable to tear my eyes away from the rusty fender of an onrushing truck. On another day I wanted to ride away from the stench that arises from slum alleys—the peculiar stink that comes from the mingling of stale *pulque*, dried blood, *frijole* farts and piss, from the strange odors only found in the tropics of lava dust carried by the wind across old sex and decomposing corpses. Chilies and sunburnt flesh, volcanoes surrounding the city and always threatening cataclysm, the blood-drenched soil of that tortured, long-suffering nation—one thinks that even Mexico's history stinks.

In 1957 I was twenty-three years old, a wandering, pot-smoking poet on a quest. I wanted to discover unknown places, find a remote spot, go where no other gringo had ever gone, past the last missionary outpost, to an area free from all contamination by Western culture, Western people, Western things. I was filled with the spirit of adventure, and I had a plan.

I believed that missionaries were the first people to reach the uncharted regions, so I thought all I had to do was find out where the most remote missionary outpost was and from there begin my journey into the unknown. It turned out that in the 1950s there were a number of cases reported of missionaries being killed by Indians in South and Central America. The missionaries responded by becoming more cautious. Now, before entering any area considered dangerous, they would flood the region with transistor radios and flashlights, using converted Indians to distribute these gifts. They hoped that these things would tranquilize the hostile savages so that when they entered the area to evangelize they would not be killed. I soon discovered that the palliative tran-

Fig. 2.1. On the road to Paititi

sistor radios and flashlights were ubiquitous. It was difficult indeed to find any place where these symbols of Western ways had not yet made their appearance.

After long trial and error I devised a method for reaching the most remote areas that still remained. I was in the state of Oaxaca when one day I decided to take a second-class bus to the end of the line. On the outskirts of the last town I found a road that apparently led into the mountains and I walked that road for seven days and then returned to where I had started. For two years I pursued this method of travel. Each of the towns at the end of the second-class bus line would always have a narrow road on its outskirts and each and every one of these roads had one thing in common. They all led nowhere.

I found this method of travel exhilarating. I was freed from the need of choosing a destination. I would know where I was going when I got there. Every road I traveled was a new adventure. I always asked the people living in these last-stop towns where the road went, and invariably they answered, "Nowhere." So then I asked if anyone in town had ever traveled on that road and they would answer, "No one travels the road. No one ever has a reason to go to such a godforsaken place. Only Indians use those roads, and damn few of them." And I found it was true; the roads were very lightly traveled. Sometimes I would pass an Indian walking in the opposite direction and occasionally they would ask me where I was heading. It was the only question they ever asked. To every one of them I gave the same reply, "I'll know where I'm going when I get there." And the beautiful thing is I never met an Indian who thought that answer strange. To the Indians it made good sense.

Eventually I would arrive at some isolated house, some ranch or village baking beneath a late-afternoon tropical sun. I would always be treated kindly by the people, offered food and a mat to sleep on for the night. In the morning I would arise early, thank my hosts for their generosity, and tell them I was leaving to continue on that road that went nowhere. They were always surprised but much too polite to ask why. When they saw I was serious about leaving on my journey, they would stop me and give me this advice: "It is always good to go in peace, but not without a gun." And so I asked them what lay beyond their village on this endless mountain path I was following. They would assure me that the next two villages were quite all right, inhabited by decent people like themselves. But beyond the second village lived evil people with bad intentions. Bandits and assassins, all. No one ever ventured there without a guide who had strong connections through friends or family to those thieving murderers. And even then they insisted that no sane man, even if he went in peace, should go without a gun.

Against the well-intentioned warnings of these kindly Indians I continued walking the road. When I passed the second village and continued onward into the land of the supposed killers and thieves, I found the people to be as kindly and generous as the people who warned me not to go there.

The farther I walked on the road that went nowhere the more I saw that it was not only distance that separated me from the great urban centers but, more important, time. Walking those roads was like moving backwards through the centuries. In those places nothing had changed for hundreds of years. So onward I marched past ranches and villages and sometimes again I would be warned about the people ahead and those people ahead would always be just like the people behind me. No matter how far I traveled these roads, I never managed to reach the end of the line. One day while walking it occurred to me that I must be somewhere since I was aware of both myself and my surroundings. But if I had to tell someone else who had never been there where I was, the best description I could think of would be to say that it was nowhere.

And yes, I did reach places free from flashlights and transistor radios, but there were three things I could never get beyond: Coca-Cola, Singer sewing machines, and pool tables. It was maddening. These three things penetrated everywhere. I called them the Unholy Trinity and I vowed that no matter how far I had to go or how difficult the trail might be, I would reach some place beyond that horrible trio. A town or a village still free from Coca-Cola, sewing machines, and pool tables. But was it possible? Was there anyplace left within the borders of the Mexican republic that still remained uncontaminated? Or was it a fantasy, a dream, like Ponce de León seeking the fountain of youth or Spanish conquistadors searching everywhere for the seven lost cities of Cibola? Whether it was real or not didn't matter. I would go on looking until I walked off the edge of the earth, till my face turned cherry red. I must find it. It was like a pain in the foundation of my being, like the maddening sensation of an unscratchable itch. To make it a concrete reality in my mind, I must give it a name. I called it Paititi, after the legendary living city of the Incas that fearless explorers still search for in Peru.

In search of Paititi my soul must go. Beyond the last known port of call, along a coast of deserted seasons under unrecorded skies. Outside the ancient realm of time, past the last unconquered border in the undiscovered mountains of the mind. A journey for life that sometimes begins at the instant of death as infinity collapses upon itself, relinquishing sovereignty over flesh. In a system within a system within a system, in a dream that spirals toward the light as the universal energy transforms and is refined, I move freely beyond the edge of macrocosmic limitations and am aware that orange is but the brilliance of blue made incandescent in a pig iron crucible of magnetized constellations reflecting no eternal cancer, exposing no galactic destination, no horizon of perfect truth. Wisdom speaks by the green light of hummingbirds, in the archaic tongue of trees. And many who seek it are forever lost in the lustrous ache of forgotten sensations, in childhood Decembers, in the bittersweet taste of yesterday's disheveled rains. Lost without exit and lost without hope under a shadow of fractured eclipses, in the winter's unharvested shade, in some marinated angle, some secret perspective, some hidden trapezoid, some mechanized equator or occulted wrinkle on the invisible longitude of madness in money's frozen smile. Lost in explosions of endless expansions . . . in the gullies and canyons of time.*

I opened my large map of Oaxaca. I must choose a region that had the greatest possibility. Three areas looked promising. On the eastern side of the state lay the Sierra Mazateca, in the center is the Mixteca Alta, and in the northwest a large region bordering Guerrero state called the Ex District of Putla. Putla was my choice. I couldn't resist the name.

---

* This entire paragraph is a prose form of Marty's poem "In Search of Paititi," published in *Time Waits: Selected Poems 1956–1986* and also recorded on the CD of Marty's poetry, *A Sky of Fractured Feathers* (New York: Fang Records, 2001).

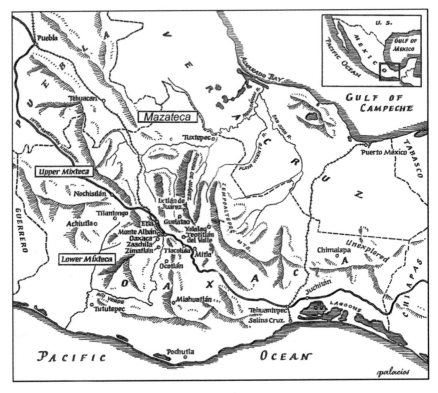

Fig. 2.2. The state of Oaxaca, Mexico

Running through the district were high mountains I called the Sierra de Putla Madre. I set out.[*]

For me those were times when life was filled with rich flavor. I still recall scenes from nights heavy with magic as if I were still there. Evenings, perhaps when the moon was rising, lying in a hammock under a sky filled with more stars than grains of sand in the ocean, cradling a good bottle of Mescal in which one could see the embalmed carcass of a fat cactus worm. From some invisible jackal would come the sound of a well-strummed guitar filling the air with its pulsating rhythm, and the skeletal village mongrels would begin howling their canine lamentations.

---

[*] The fact that Marty's description can be reconstructed and mapped indicates his ability to remember details many years after being first introduced to them and invites intrepid explorers to reconstruct his steps.

When the moon goddess Metztli cleared the horizon and became a fat luminous eye looking down upon her dark dominion, even the most logical minds, those skeptics trained in the latest scientific methods and techniques, could not state with certainty that out there just beyond vision there were no shapeshifters, no *duendes*, no *tloques*, no enchanted dwarfs or, just perhaps, more sinister powers. For the night was their time and only the greatest of fools would deny it.

As the hours passed and the bottle slowly emptied down my throat into my stomach, my mind became clear. The fermented cactus unshackled my poetic spirit and nurtured my soul. Ah, the mystery of the Soul! I heard a voice in the night call out, "Como Mexico no hay dos" (Oh Mexico, there aren't two). Under my breath I whispered, "Gracias a Dios" (Thanks be to God). And in my mind I wondered if there was really even one.

At the turn of the century when the cacique of all caciques, don Porfírio Diaz, ruled Mexico with his paternal smile and his iron fist, he was asked what Mexico's biggest problem was. He replied, "Poor Mexico. So far from God and so close to the United States!" For me, however, the old dictator, though not lacking in wit, had it completely backwards. To my way of thinking, Mexico is closer to God by far than it is to the U.S. border.

I shall put aside these pleasant ruminations and return to the tale of my travels. The more I studied my map of Oaxaca the more certain I became in my mind that there, in the district of Putla, I would find my Paititi. I would at last reach a village beyond Coca-Cola, sewing machines, and pool tables. And for a change I had chosen a destination in advance even if it was a large area and not a specific town.

Now economics also began to play a part in my travels. In my life I have known only two economic situations—rapidly running out of money and completely out of money. At this point I was rapidly running out of money but I thought I could hold out long enough to reach my goal. I felt that Paititi was within my grasp. To be poor in Mexico was no shame; to be in a state of poverty was to be one among many millions.

As rapidly as I could, I walked to a town where a second-class bus made its last stop. From there I rode on a series of buses until I reached Pinotepa National, a virtual metropolis of 4,000 souls. In Pinotepa National I was fortunate to make contact with a rancher who agreed to rent me a horse for four days at ten pesos a day, payable in advance. He showed me a trail and told me four days' ride would bring me to a cattle ranch owned by a friend of his, don Rodrigo Arnulfo Boza, the richest and most powerful cacique in that area of the Sierra. He wrote a letter of introduction to don Rodrigo for me and told me to leave the horse I was renting at Rodrigo's when I left to continue onward. He explained that from that point onward I would have to continue by foot because a river ran through his friend's ranch that could only be crossed by a hammock bridge which no animal, be it horse, mule, or burro, could pass over.

My ten-peso-a-day transportation was a small, brown, stupid mountain horse I called Pendejo (coward) when I found it necessary to call him anything. The saddle was nothing more than unpadded wood. The stirrups could not be adjusted and were, of course, much too short. These things resulted in a locked knee and a very sore ass. And need I add that when I finally arrived at don Rodrigo's ranch my letter of introduction was totally useless because Rodrigo couldn't read a word? Viva México! I loved it.

Upon my arrival at Rodrigo's I was exhausted, sore, stiff, and starving. I decided to rest and recuperate before continuing. A short time after introducing myself and exchanging the minimal pleasantries required by polite Spanish custom, I excused myself and retreated to the shade of a Zapote tree outside the ranch house.

I carefully trickled the languid afternoon through my fingers. I looked at the Mexican sky, which was always filled with buzzards, just as the Mexican land is always drenched in death, always well adorned with carcasses and corpses. In this nation where hunger is endemic, the scavenger feeds best. The vulture never needs to look far for a meal, for Dr. Death not only resides in Mexico, he spends most of his time there too. Life seems thin and has a frail hold where so many die in so many ways without apparent reason, without justice or cause, by whim or luck, by God's will or by stray bullets. So death transcends itself, becomes art, philosophy, celebration, and a ritual as well as an escape from the prison where those sentenced by birth spend their time. In Mexico wealth and property have far greater value than life. "La vida no vale una chingada," as they say. Life ain't worth a fuck.

Now in the more remote areas of Mexico, such as in the Sierra de Putla Madre, men still dressed in loose white pants and the shirts of peons—the clothing that one commonly sees in old photographs of the revolution. These campesinos and Indians who work for the hacienda owners and caciques labor under the peonage system, a form of slavery. Poverty was so severe and widespread that starvation was not an uncommon cause of death.

If the people were literally starving, imagine the condition of domestic animals. Mangy skeletal dogs without hair, skin covered with sores erupting pus, slinked through the shadows, searching for any edible morsel. They had stiff competition from even uglier pigs who somehow retained the strength to remain bad tempered and hostile and dangerous to all other living things. The adults were extremely large and almost hairless, with gray, leprous skin. They looked more reptilian than mammalian. Only their tusks looked healthy. Taking a shit when they were nearby required cunning, planning, dexterity, and agility. They were so hungry they would charge a squatting man to get at the stool before it even hit the ground. This meant you had to find a mound or a boulder to protect your back while relieving yourself. It was also necessary to gather a large number of stones to hurl at the pigs to keep them at bay until you finished. Nothing that came from the human asshole, from iron-hard constipated turds to liquid pools of diarrhea, remained on the ground for even sixty seconds. Those porkers ate it all. In fact, those swine ate feces of all kinds. They would eat anything they could swallow, and I mean anything, with only one exception. They wouldn't eat their own shit. Who could blame them? Nothing would.

After two days of restful recuperation I crossed the swinging hammock bridge, leaving the ranch behind. On the river's far side the path climbed steeply and continued to rise for two and a half more days until just before the summit I reached another village. Along that trail were places so narrow, so steep, so difficult to pass, it seemed only a mountain goat with miraculous luck could negotiate them and manage to reach that tiny town. It was small. It had no store. Nothing was sold there. Nonetheless, the first house I entered had not only some empty Coke bottles, but an antique treadle-powered Singer sewing machine that no longer worked. In a hut where no one lived, an ancient pool table sat. I was beaten, unable to even imagine any means by which that table had gotten to where I had barely managed to climb. I bowed my head in surrender. I refused to speculate further. I refused to ask anyone how it had arrived where it was. Only a magic carpet or an act of God could have transported that table to that hut.

This was the end. I was now completely out of money and bone tired. I would have to continue without finding my Paititi, the place beyond the reach of the Unholy Trio. Coke, Foot Treadle, and Eight Ball went where no explorer, no missionary, no angel had ever gone before. So be it.

The following morning, as I was leaving, an old white-haired Indian joined me on the path. His wrinkled face seemed coffee stained, his eyes luminous and wise. After greeting each other formally, he introduced himself.

"Onofre Sandoval, a su servicio." (At your service.)

I told him my name in return and asked if he was walking far.

"I'm going to the store of Antonio, the one-eyed Spaniard."

"Store?" I asked, amazed. "Is it far?"

"Only about four hours' easy walking," Onofre replied.

We proceeded in silence for a while, but curiosity prompted me to ask what Antonio, the one-eyed Spaniard, sold in his establishment.

"Aguardiente, cigarros, refrescos, y cerveza cuando hay, lata de sardina y galletas salados. Nada mas." (Cane alcohol, cigarettes, soft drinks and beer when he has them, cans of sardines and salt crackers. Nothing else.)

"How can he make enough to live on with so little for sale in such a remote location?"

"He grows his corn, of course, and a few other things. His house is conveniently located about equal distance from three tiny villages. So he sells a bit now and then. But up here, those of us who have been blessed with good fortune live in poverty most of the time and there is little money to spend. I myself have been poor most of my life, but not for long. No," he repeated, "not for long."

I had been saving my last cigarettes carefully and still had almost half a pack. I offered one to Onofre, which he accepted with gratitude, and I took one myself. I thought about what he said about being poor most of his life but "not for long." And I wondered what he meant. To question him on such a short acquaintanceship would have been rude and extremely ill-mannered. The curious mind, however, will not remain still but insists on being satisfied in some fashion. Even if I could not ask what I wished, my mind considered possibilities as we walked. Could he have children who worked in a city, or even in the United States, who made money that he expected them to send? Could he have discovered some buried treasure in his cornfield, hidden during the revolution? Did he have dreams about winning the national lottery? And so on and so forth. My speculations ran on, hand in hand with my imagination, producing increasingly ingenious solutions.

The sun had not yet reached its zenith when we arrived at the little store of Antonio, the one-eyed Spaniard. It was none too soon. I was tired, hungry, and needed to rest. Suddenly a gloomy cloud seemed to descend. I was overcome with a feeling of deep depression. My long quest had failed when I had been sure it would succeed. Furthermore, I was about to enter the only store I had seen for many days and I was not likely to see another for many more. And I didn't even have money to buy a can of sardines and some salt crackers, which at that moment seemed like a royal banquet that I desperately wanted to eat.

As we entered Antonio's hut, Onofre pulled a large bandana out of his pocket, the corners tied together to make a bag.

"Good morning don Antonio," said Onofre. "Give me a pack of Farolitos" ("little lighthouses," Mexico's cheapest brand of cigarettes).

He untied his bandana on the counter. Within it lay three copper coins—a twenty, a ten, and a five centavo piece. It was obviously the only money in the world that was his.

And as he handed over his last thirty-five centavos, I understood what he had meant when he said he was poor but not for long. Truly, he spoke for both of us when he said as he paid, "Sacavo la pobreza, empieza la miseria"—Good-bye poverty, here comes misery.

And so ends the tale of Marty's search for Paititi. It seems unfinished, but then again, it ends definitively enough. The last anecdote indicates that beyond poverty lies misery. In a spiritual sense, when we give away our last valuable thing, poverty is gone and misery, the beginning of spiritual suffering, truly sets in. The quest inevitably leads to a full desertion of every last possession of selfhood, including our illusions about the real nature of the quest, and this is the prelude to being filled with something beyond the concerns and possessions of the ego. This is a major theme in the spiritual meaning of the Pyramid of Fire. Although Marty's story ends here, we can presume that Paititi was not found in the Sierra de Putla Madre. A realization occurred to Marty, however, that he carried with him on his later adventures into the Sierra Madre de Mazateca: the realization that after our final illusion is unveiled, our journey really begins.

In our conversations Marty referred to the region of Ayauhtla as a paradise. We can rightly conclude that the discovery of the Pyramid of Fire was the culmination of his Mexican quest, of his search for Paititi, the realm beyond the touch of Westernization. For the Pyramid of Fire comes from a time before the invaders from the east arrived.

We have already sketched Marty's activities in Mexico, and this short story has provided an autobiographical picture of his first years there. For continuity in preserving Marty's vision of what the Pyramid of Fire means, we can now move directly to a more fictional narrative, an unfinished novella that Marty wrote in 1995. It will prepare us for a full reading of the text of the codex in chapter 4.

The Pyramid of Fire
A Novella

Whereas the short story "In Search of Paititi" can be considered autobiographical, Marty's unfinished novella is in the fiction-allegory genre (Marty called it a "fantasy-adventure"). Despite this fictional basis, however, deeper meanings regarding the teachings in the Pyramid of Fire can be gleaned from this work.

Part 1

Because that which is above created that which is below
and that which is low reflects that which is high,
the universe is Tezcatlipoca, Smoking Mirror,
in which man still does not see clearly.

PYRAMID OF FIRE, 2:14–17

My name is Mark Stevens, and the story I am about to relate will be believed by few. For many years I was an archaeologist and student of magic. I traveled extensively in South and Central America, especially in Mexico, where I made my living dealing in Pre-Columbian art objects. Adventures too numerous to relate here occurred over many years, during which I rambled down hidden trails and lived in remote villages for months at a time. I learned some of the local Indian dialects, and fate brought me to a Mazatec Indian village called Ayauhtla in the state of Oaxaca. I had been hired by a collector in Mexico City to search for some clay figures associated with the Mazatec mushroom cult, and upon arriving in the village a series of connections eventually led me to the house of Daniel Flores Flores, a local *brujo*, a medicine shaman. Daniel Flores Flores was a true man of power, a healer, a finder, a caster of spells, a shape changer, and a seer of extraordinary reputation able to see into both the past and future.*

After I had been visiting Ayauhtla for three years running, don Daniel showed me the ancient Nahuatl codex called the Pyramid of Fire, and gave me a necklace of rock crystal skulls. He told me that I was the one he had been waiting for and that if I chose to, I could travel back in time almost five hundred years. He told me that this must be accomplished through a combination of his Indian magic and the magic of my own culture.

One thing was essential for the plan to go forward: I would need a wand of power. Now, based on my own studies in the magical arts—from medieval books known as *grimoires*—I knew a wand of power should be manufactured in the following way: On the night of a full moon a goat is sacrificed and the blood of the animal is allowed to stay on the sacrificial knife. Next, a fresh, virgin hazel branch must be found (virgin in the sense that the tree is less than a year old and has never been cut). The branch is set aside and is not touched during the day it is found. The next morning at sunrise the branch is cut with the sacrificial knife, and its length must be exactly nineteen and one-half inches. As the branch is cut an invocation is spoken, such as this one from Great Albert's *Grimoirium Verum*:

> I invoke Thee, O great Adonai, Eloim, Ariel, and Jehovam, grant Thy beneficence and endow this rod I am cutting with the power and virtue of Jacob, Moses, and the great Joshua. I invoke you to place in this wand the strength of Samson, the anger of Emmanuel, and the thunder and lightning of Zariatnakmek—he who will

---

* If this sounds eerily like the don Juan of Castaneda, we should recall that Castaneda modeled his shaman on the ethnographic accounts of Myerhoff's don Ramon (recounted in her book *Peyote Hunt*, 44–49). In other words, the similarity derives from a common archetypal vocation, that of a pan-Nagualism stretching from the Yaqui desert of northern Mexico into Honduras. —*JMJ*

avenge the sins and crimes of men on the Great Day of Judgment. Amen.*

After the invocation and the cutting are finished, the magician looks toward the sun and takes the wand into his room. The next step calls for steel caps to be fitted to each end of the wand. The text insists that the wand be shown to no one until its construction is complete. The steel caps are procured in this manner: The still-bloody sacrificial knife and two pieces of wood the size of the ends of the wand are taken to a blacksmith. He fashions the caps out of the knife to the size of the wood pieces. These are then fitted to the wand. A piece of lodestone is passed over the two ends for magnetizing, while a final invocation is spoken:

> By the Greatest Adonai, Eloim, Ariel, and Jehovam, I command you to grant all that I desire by the supreme power of the great Adonai, Eloim, and Jehovam, and I invoke Thee by the incompatibility of fire and water to separate all things as they were separated on the great Day of Creation. Amen.

Finally, using gilt or golden ink the magician paints a number of words, Hebrew letters, and esoteric symbols on the wand. Toward the handle he writes *Ego* and *Alpha et Omega*, and on the opposite side Adonai; in the middle write Tetragrammaton; at the tip Agla.

That is how it needed to be done. Working with a priest-magician whom I had located after careful searches, I forged my magic wand, and this was my contribution to the journey that don Daniel invited me to take. The Hebrew letters and symbols that I used must remain my secret.†

---

* Marty wrote both this and the following invocations. They are loosely based upon but not quoted verbatim from the *Grimoirium Verum,* often attributed to Albertus Magnus and available for viewing online at: www.hermetics.org/pdf/Grimoirium_Verum.pdf.

† Because Daniel asked "Mark Stevens" to contribute something from "his own culture," the implication here is that Stevens is Jewish. Marty himself was of Jewish background, and it is probable that Marty indicates here that the Pyramid of Fire, being an expression of the perennial philosophy, parallels esoteric teachings found everywhere, including even elements of popular magic in medieval grimoires. Marty repeatedly emphasized that the Pyramid of Fire codex contains tarot and Kabbalah symbolism, the Kabbalah being the best-known expression of Jewish mysticism. —*JMJ*

The end of January approached. Soon it would be time for the journey to begin. Don Daniel had been spending the evenings going forth as a jaguar, his Nagual. A Nagual is a guardian spirit that takes the form of an animal or bird and presides over a man's fate. It is believed that the animal spirit companion is joined with a newborn baby and stays with it throughout its life. If the Nagual is lost, it is seen as a soul loss and the person will soon die unless a shaman can retrieve the lost spirit. The belief in Nagualism is ancient and was found throughout the Americas at the time of the Spanish conquest of Mexico. Unfortunately, Nagualism was quickly demonized by the newcomers.

Antonio de Herrera, in his general history, wrote of Honduran Nagualists active in 1530, "The devil deluded them, and appeared in the shape of a crocodile, a serpent, or a bird, which they called Naguales, signifying guardians, and when the animal or bird died the Indian who was in league with them also died, which often happened." The contract with a Nagual could be initiated at birth or in the following way:

> . . . the Indian went into the wilderness and called upon the devils they worshipped as Gods, and talked to the river, the rocks, or the woods, and sacrificed a dog or a cock to them. He then went to sleep, and either in a dream or when he awoke he would see one of the before mentioned creatures or birds and would beg of it to grant an alliance, drawing blood with a thorn from his own tongue, ears, or other parts of the body, thereby sealing a contract with the beast. And this animal in a dream or awake would tell him, "On such a day you shall go walking, and I shall be the first bird or animal you will encounter, and from that day on I shall be your Nagual and companion at all times." Whereupon such friendship was contracted between them, such that when one of them died the other did not survive.[1]

Another example of Nagualism is given by Francisco Fuentes y Guzman in his history of Guatemala, written about 1690. He relates a story of a sorcerer from Totonicapan in the western highlands of

Guatemala who was arrested by the Inquisition and questioned as to how a proper Nagual was assigned to a child. He gave this account:

> When informed of the day of birth, he [the shaman-daykeeper] went to the house of the parents and, taking the child outside, he invoked the demon. Then he unfolded one of their books of pictures, a divinatory calendar which had next to each day an animal or object. Upon selecting the correct animal or object which corresponded to the day of birth, he would complete the invocation and the Nagual would appear. He would then address this Nagual and pray, requesting it to protect the child and accompany it through life."[2]

The Popol Vuh, sometimes called the Mayan Bible, speaks of one of the great musician kings of the Quiché Maya, stating that Gucumatz, the wizard monarch, could transform himself into a serpent, an eagle, a jaguar, and even lower forms of life. This indicates that a magician could transform himself into the form of his Nagual or other animals, an ability called shapeshifting.

But shapeshifting was not the only magical resource of a true shaman such as don Daniel. The Nagualist's arts were manifold. They could become invisible and walk unseen among their enemies. They could transport themselves to distant places and return, reporting all that they had witnessed. Before the eyes of spectators they could create rivers, trees, houses, animals, and other objects. To all appearances they could rip themselves open, cut a limb from the body of another person and replace it, or pierce themselves with knives without bleeding. They could handle poisonous snakes without being bitten or invoke spirits who would instantly appear. But by transforming himself into a Nagual, a shaman leaves himself vulnerable to his enemies. Traveling in this form can be very dangerous. When a Nagual dies, so does the man. Yet only certain men, true men, men of power, can transform themselves into their Naguals. And as don Daniel himself has said, "What man of power has no enemies?"

It was late afternoon. Daniel and I were sitting in front of his house, smoking and watching the shadows fall across the mushroom meadows. I looked down the steep slopes of the rich green mountainside to where it fell away among the tumbled rocks and the roaring Santa Domingo River disappeared into the mist on its rushing journey to join the Great River of Butterflies (Rio Papaloapan) in Veracruz State.

"Don Daniel," I asked, "why go out tonight as a jaguar? You have been taking many chances lately."

"The time is at hand," he replied, "and I must speak with the ancestors. I must enlist their aid and ask for certain instructions. This I can do only in my Nagual form. Also, I must find where the *derrumbes* (sacred mushrooms) grow, for this is not their season and they are essential. I may have to look far and move fast, and this too is best done in the jaguar form. Tomorrow, Marco, you must begin to fast in preparation and at dawn we leave for the sacred mushroom journey-caves on Cerro Rabon. There, certain things must be done before we proceed further. Now ask no more questions; I must concentrate to be ready for this evening."

And don Daniel must have ventured far and wide that evening while I slept in a dreamless deep.

On the following morning, just before the break of day, don Daniel roused me from the sleeping mat. "It is time," he said, "we must go."

I followed him out of the hut and into the chill obsidian dark. It was about five o'clock. I looked up at the stars, brilliant chips of pulsating ice, and then toward the east where fingers of deep purple were beginning to stain the tops of the mountains. Daniel picked up a large *costal* (woven sack) and threw it over his shoulder as I followed him through the winding streets of Ayauhtla. In a few minutes the light became stronger. The Morning Star seemed to flee before an invisible wind, then disappear like a crystal dropped into clear water. The houses began to show up, scattered haphazardly across the mountain's shoulder—strong oblongs of adobe roofed with thatch, bowed at the top and overhanging the edges in such a way that they resembled Chinese pagodas. Some seemed to rise ghostlike from the early morning mist.

We climbed along the steep dirt path. Wildflowers grew in magnificent clusters. Waterfalls raced down the mountainside and splashed across the trail at our feet, then continued on downward into what seemed like the fields of infinity itself. Rainbow-colored rocks were every-where. I felt wonderful. I was walking on air, as if through the pages of a fairy tale. At any moment I expected to round a bend and see a turreted castle or a dragon. On we marched, higher and higher, and as the day wore on it became hotter. Don Daniel never paused and even though he was carrying his large costal, I was hard put to keep up with him.

At about two o'clock in the afternoon we reached the pass at the top, where we stopped to catch our breath. A cool breeze was blowing, drying our sweat. From this pass it is possible to see a long way, and the view was incredible. In front of us, down below, the tropical vegetation grew lux-uriant and thick. On the far side of the pass was a mountain shaped like a hunchback, easily distinguished from all the others nearby. At the top of this curious mountain was another pass, guarded by two giant stone eagles. Don Daniel, who had been silent the whole trip, pointed to the hunchback mountain and said, "Cerro Rabon. There lies the sacred mushroom caves." And without another word, he picked up his burden and off we went again.

It was about eight o'clock in the evening when we finally reached the cave, about three quarters of the way up Cerro Rabon. It was already dark, but even in daylight it would have been almost impossible to spot the entrance. Obscured by two trees growing a few yards in front of it, the portal was just large enough to crawl into. Yet this was the entrance into an inner world of huge dimension, larger than I could even suspect at that moment. Just inside, where the diffuse starlight mingled with cool breezes, we set out our blankets and drank some water. I was exhausted and went to sleep at once.

In the morning don Daniel took me deeper into the cave, where it opened into a great chamber. At the far side of the chamber a tunnel opening led directly into the heart of the mountain. With two old miner's lamps fastened to our heads, we ventured into the tunnel. I could see a series of petroglyphs on the left—very archaic looking. As we continued onward, we began to gradually descend. On the right-hand side of the tunnel wall I saw a series of seven heads, each with a mushroom sprout-ing from the top. The passageway descended for perhaps two hundred yards, until it opened into another large chamber at the rear of which I could see openings to three more tunnels. Don Daniel went straight to the tunnel on the left-hand side, and I heard him begin to say a prayer. He then chanted words that echoed the same teachings in the ancient picture book he had shown me:

> Man climbs the tree of life between Tonatiuh, the Sun,
> and Mictlantecuhtli, Lord of the Hells and of Death.
> At the foot of the tree that grows between the symbols
> that represent earth, air, water, and fire,
> the constituent parts that intervened in his conception
> are reunited: the semen with which his parents engendered him,
> the pig of personality, the eagle of spirit,
> and in a basket spotted with stars, the bones of mortality
> and the wings of the soul.
> The summit of the tree is Death where shines the Sun itself,
> the Midnight Sun from which radiate the four paths or ways.
> From here surge the wings of the soul finally liberated,
> while above, each of his various parts, separated by death,
> runs to its destiny.
> To the left, to the fields of Death, goes the corpse draped in flesh,
> the beast that returns to the root of the tree.
> To the right, to the side of Life, goes the serpent of consciousness
> that came from the sun and to the sun returns,
> the spirit by which man is transfigured in the stellar world.
> And over all, the Milky Way of innumerable suns.

We crawled into the tunnel and very soon, just before it opened into the largest of all the chambers we had yet encountered, I saw the twenty day signs of the Aztec calendar carved into the solid stone of the cave. The table on page 41 indicates what these signs look like and provides their Aztec and English names.

At this point I should briefly sketch the workings of the Aztec calendar so that the reader will understand what is to follow.

There are two different calendar cycles that intermesh with each other. The solar calendar consists of eighteen months of twenty days

THE TWENTY AZTEC DAY SIGNS

AZTEC GLYPH	AZTEC NAME	ENGLISH NAME
	Cipactli	Crocodile
	Ehecatl	Wind God
	Calli	House
	Cuetzpallin	Lizard
	Coatl	Serpent
	Miquiztli	Death
	Mazatl	Deer
	Tochtli	Rabbit
	Atl	Water
	Itzcuintli	Dog
	Ozomatli	Monkey
	Malinalli	Twisted Grass
	Acatl	Reed
	Ocelotl	Tiger/Jaguar
	Cuauhtli	Eagle
	Cozaquauhtli	Vulture
	Ollin	Earthquake/Movement
	Tecpatl	Flint Knife
	Quiahuitl	Rain
	Xochitl	Flower

each, equaling 360 days, plus a five-day month at the end to make a total of 365 days. This is the secular or mundane calendar. Then there is the sacred or divinatory calendar, the Tonalamatl (Book of Days), consisting of thirteen periods of twenty days, totaling 260 days. The intermeshing of these two cycles, one sacred and one mundane, generates a period called a Calendar Round, which is just a little less than 52 solar years. During this time, no date ever repeats. Here is the math:

$$260 \times 73 = 365 \times 52 = 18,980 \text{ days}$$

Due to the peculiarities of the interworkings of these two calendars, each year can begin on one of only four of the sacred day signs. In the Aztec system they are: Calli (House), Tochtli (Rabbit), Acatl (Reed), and Tecpatl (Flint Knife). Each one of these four day signs is associated with one of the four quarters of the world, or cardinal points of the compass: Acatl is East, Tecpatl is North, Calli is West, and Tochtli is South. Colors, gods, and elements are also associated with the four world quarters. In the East we find the color yellow, the Goddess of Terrestrial Waters (Chalchiuhtlicue), and the element water. In the North we have the God of Death (Mictlantecuhtli), the color white, and the element earth. West is associated with the color red, the element air, and the Goddess Itzpapálotl, who, as the Obsidian Butterfly, is an aspect of Venus. Finally, in the South we find the color blue, the element fire, and Itzpalpotec, the God of Sacrifice.*

The Ancients believed that the supreme divinity, Tloque Nahuaque, manifests as Ometecuhtli, the God of Duality, and functions through a principle of dynamic dualism or polarity. We call the two forces of this principle *active* and *passive,* or *masculine* and *feminine,* but this duality can function only by interacting against a neutral background and thus the two become three. This trinity then produces the four prime elements: air, earth, fire, and water (symbolizing space, energy, time, and matter), and through them the whole material world is engendered. Such was the cosmovision of the ancient Aztecs and Mazatecs, don Daniel's ancestors.

---

* Marty took these associations directly from the Pyramid of Fire; there were regional variations in deity associations that occurred during the dispersion of the calendar systems. —*JMJ*

It was now the last day in January. Through the manipulation of the sacred symbols, by the magical blessing of the sacred mushrooms and with the aid of the wand of power, we hoped to travel back in time. Our launch date—or as it turned out, *my* launch date—was set for February 2 for two reasons: First, it was New Year's Day in the Aztec calendar. Second, it was Candlemas Eve, a seasonal cross-quarter, one of the four nights of the year when the powers of sorcery and magical invocation were strongest, according to Western witchcraft.

As we entered the large chamber just beyond the day glyphs at the end of the last tunnel, don Daniel put down his costal and looked at me.

"Marco," he said, "at the far side of this chamber is an abyss which in ancient days was crossed by a log bridge. On the other side you will find a rope ladder that descends ninety meters to the opening of another tunnel. This tunnel leads to another exit that overlooks a huge space in which you will see a moon pyramid. Remember, you must leave only by that exit. This is the first part of the initiation into the sacred mushroom mysteries. Go into that space and approach the moon pyramid. There you will be met. I have already spoken with the ancestors, and they will be waiting.

"Now, Marco, we must make plans. You must continue your fast and later today, when we leave these chambers, you will ritually purify yourself in the *temizcal* (steam bath). Use the one located a short distance from where we first entered the cave. Now, pay attention! Here is the date you must concentrate on: 1 Reed, 7 Movement. While I am chanting, you must focus all your thoughts on that date, 1 Reed, 7 Movement. This will send you to the right time. Now explain to me your magic circle."

In addition to my wand of power, the magic circle was my other contribution to the ceremony. Since ancient times the circle has been one of the primary tools of Western magic.

"The shape of the circle is perfect," I explained. "It is the only shape in nature in which every point along the perimeter is an equal distance from the center. It represents the oneness of all things in relation to their source. Within itself it contains both the beginning and the end, and is thus a graphic symbol of the cyclic nature of time and of resurrection or rebirth. At the same time it also represents the ever-grinding wheel of existence and the endless chain of birth and death to which man is bound. All other primary symbols—the square, the triangle, the point, the line—fit into the circle and may be enclosed there, as in a womb. Clearly the circle is a mother matrix, the Alpha and Omega, the Beginning and End, of universal design."

Don Daniel was listening intently. I continued, "In the world of Western magic, this all-encompassing symbol has a practical as well as symbolic application. Its circumference describes a closed circuit, making it both useful to protect from what is without or entrap what is within. Inside it the magician is invulnerable. The only time danger can threaten is when part of the circle is broken or accidentally destroyed. The utmost caution must be taken when drawing the magic circle. The magician can use chalk, or it may be outlined in the sand, arranged with stones, constructed with flour, sacrificial goat skin, crushed shells or human bones. In this case, I would like to use shells. Don Daniel, are there any at hand?"

"Yes," he replied. "I heard of this need in a dream, and I will have a bagful placed by the outer chamber."

"Good," I said. "The outer circle is drawn first, then an inner circle about a hand's breadth from the first is made. Next, a miniature model of the cosmos is arranged by dividing the circle into four equal sections, each representing one of the four quarters of the universe. Hebrew names are written in each quadrant for divine protection. They are: Jehovah, Tetragrammaton, Adonai, and Sadai. Further inscriptions are added along the periphery, along with mystic emblems and sayings from the Bible. I will then place whatever magic implements I need within the circle. Outside the circle a charcoal fire is kindled and incense is burned. At the end I will walk around the circle, checking to see that everything is properly prepared, then step through the ring by means of a small opening left in the circumference for this purpose. After I seal this door from within, the ritual can begin."

"All right," don Daniel said. "I see how your tradition of magic and mine will work together. They are both based on the four directions united by the central portal into the heart of time. We will begin at once to draw the circle. You wait here and I will get the shells and my costal."

After a little while don Daniel returned with all that we needed.

From one large bag he spilled a large quantity of shells and began crushing them with a rock against the floor of the cave. I took out my wand, which I had been carrying in an embroidered case slung over my shoulder by a linen strap.

Using the point of the wand, I scraped the outline of the outer circle about nine feet in diameter, being careful to leave a small opening for entering and exiting. I then repeated the process for the inner circle. The sound of the wand scraping the floor made a strange counterpoint to the crunching of the shells.

After about four hours, all was complete. Using the crushed shells, don Daniel had drawn on the inside of the double circle a cross aligned to the points of the compass. At the end of each arm he drew a circle and filled them with colored mineral earth according to the cardinal direction color scheme previously explained. Using the end of my wand, I then proceeded to draw the hieroglyphic sign for each direction in the colored circles. Don Daniel then placed four ceramic figures representing Chalchiuhtlicue, Mictlantecuhtli, Itzpapálotl, and Itzpalpotec over the appropriate year signs.

Now we were almost ready. We went outside and I spent the remainder of the day in the *temizcal* (steam bath). I emerged much refreshed, but feeling very weak. I slept well.

The following day was February 1, and we planned to start the ceremonies at about 9 o'clock in the evening with their culmination, if all went well, at midnight—the moment that Candlemas Eve entered. Don Daniel went off by himself and I spent the rest of the day relaxing, breathing deeply the fresh mountain air and drinking water as I continued my fast.

Don Daniel returned shortly before 9 o'clock carrying with him a large quantity of derrumbes wrapped in leaves. We proceeded immediately to the inner chamber, where the sacred circle was set up. Once again don Daniel retrieved things from his costal—a brazier with charcoal, some beeswax candles, and four tripod incense burners with copal. He was in a jovial mood. We joked and laughed, and I knew he was trying to relax me. It really wasn't necessary. I felt good, really loose. He lit a charcoal fire in the brazier and I rolled a couple of marijuana cigarettes mixed with two other leaves, Oja de Pastora and San Pablo, both good for precipitating and intensifying the mushroom high. I then chewed and swallowed a quantity of a leaf I knew as San Pedro, another preparatory compliment to the mushrooms.

At this point don Daniel lit the incense burners, took out the package of freshly picked derrumbes, and began shaking out the clumped up soil from between the stalks over the copal fire. While doing this, he made a rhythmic hissing sound over the mushrooms: "Shh, shh, shh, la, shh, shh," and so on. I put out my hands, forming a bowl, and he filled them full of mushrooms. I ate them slowly. They were fresh and almost tasteless, just slightly acrid or metallic. I took off all my clothing. Don Daniel placed the necklace of rock crystal skulls over my head. Naked, carrying the magic wand of power and a supply of candles and flint, I stepped into the ring, closed the circle, and lay down. My head pointed north and my feet to the south, with my arms extended to the sides in the crucifix position. Don Daniel seated himself cross-legged outside the circle near the brazier. He started singing softly while hitting two sticks together:

> *Click, click, click, shh, shh, shh, la, la,*
> *shh, shh, shh, click, click, click,*
> *East, the place where the light emerges.*
> *Shh, shh, shh.*
> *South, the place where death comes.*
> *Click, click, click.*
> *West, the region of the holy seed ground.*
> *Shh, shh, shh.*
> *North, the land of thorns.*
> *Click, Click, Click.*
> *In the year and in the day*
> *of obscurity and utter darkness,*
> *before there were days and years,*
> *the world in deep obscurity,*
> *all was chaos and confusion.*
> *Shh, shh, shh, click, click, click.*

Awaken! Already the sky is tinged with red,
already the dawn has come,
already the flame-colored pheasants are singing,
the fire-colored swallows.
Already butterflies are on the wing.
Shh, shh, shh, clack, clack.

The singing went on and on. At first I felt nothing but the cold. Then I became aware of a tingling electric sensation running along my skin, and my hair stood on end. I focused my mind, concentrating . . . 1 Reed, 7 Movement. The chanting picked me up like an ocean tide of bursting, colored bubbles, carrying me along to I knew not where. My inner mind resonated with the chant: 1 Reed, 7 Movement. The cold and the singing faded in and out . . . 1 Reed, 7 Movement . . . 1 Reed, 7 Movement . . . 1 Reed, 7 Movement. Don Daniel's voice shifted key:

In the place of authority,
in the place of authority we command;
it is the mandate of our principle lord,
Smoking Mirror, who makes things shine forth.
They are already on the way; they are prepared.
Intoxicate yourselves, intoxicate yourselves,
Ometecuhtli, God of Duality, is acting.
The Inventor of Man, Tezcatlipoca,
Smoking Mirror, who makes things shine forth.

Deeper stirrings welled up within me, while don Daniel continued:

Mother of the gods, Father of the gods,
the old god, distended in the navel of the earth,
engaged in the enclosure of turquoise.
He who dwells in waters the color of the bluebird,
He who dwells in the clouds, the old god.
He who inhabits the shadows of the region of the dead,
the Lord of fire and the year.

I could still clearly see the roof and walls of the cave. But then they slowly became translucent, filling with the silence of stone, fire agates and opals. They expanded, pulsing and contracting. Don Daniel's face began running like molten wax, lit by an inner glow. Age and youth, age and youth, alternately flickered. Click, click, click, 1 Reed, 7 Movement . . . 1 Reed, 7 Movement. On the walls the face of an old woman, dry, desiccated—a mummy's face showing through the bark of a tree, then jungle vegetation pushed through into focus. Softly lit abstract patterns floated through an infinity of changing forms. I saw rivers of javelins transfix the chain of time, allowing the anguished years to pause momentarily in their shackled progression. My eye opened to multitudes of hours sobbing on the broad shoulders of the rain. Even Death plays truant in the mist, secure in his mantle of gray. Click, click, click . . . 1 Reed, 7 Movement. The music went on and on . . .

Not in vain did I take the raiment of yellow plumage,
for it is I who made the sun appear.
O, portentous one, who inhabits the region of the clouds,
you have but one foot.
Inhabitor of the cold region of wings,
you have opened your hand!
Near the wall of the region that burns,
feathers come forth,
the sun spreads out,
there is a cry . . .
My God is called Protector of Men.
Oh, now he advances, comes well adorned with paper,
He who inhabits the region that burns,
in the dust, in the dust, He gyrates.

I saw red glints on the rock crystal skulls, then rainbows. The tinkling of butterfly wings. Don Daniel was there, receding through the wrong end of a telescope, then zooming in like a giant brown velvet mannequin, only to recede again. A membrane between us was dissolving into the fragmented silver strings of a benevolent spider's web. I took the wand in my right hand and touched the figure of Chalchiuhtlicue. A flash of green. The roof became transparent. Pulled outward, I passed the dancing stars in a thousand buoyant strides and grasped the joyous wind with mossy hands. 1 Reed, 7 Movement . . . 1 Reed, 7 Movement . . . click, click, click. A freezing silence . . . then, unconsciousness.

I awoke in utter blackness, and I knew instantly . . . I had made it through the barrier of time to the other side of five hundred years.

Part 2

Each world is the play of three gods,
three forces and their field of action.
As one or another god guides, as one or another god follows,
as one or another god concludes,
there can be gotten six classes of games,
six processes that create all which occurs or may occur.
These six classes of divine game decide the growth,
the decadence, the purification, the infirmity, the curation,
and the regeneration of the world.

PYRAMID OF FIRE, 4:1–9

It was cold, very cold. I was naked, I was alone, and if our calculations were correct, I was back in the year 1467, one Calendar Round before the arrival of Cortés. Montezuma the First was chief speaker in Tenochtitlan. I felt tremendously exhilarated, clearheaded, and filled with adrenaline and a fiery energy. It was pitch black, however. As I sat and sensed the world coalescing around me, I began to see, as if illuminated from my own eyes, the dim outlines of the chamber. It was empty. Gone was the magic circle, gone were the brazier, the fire, the incense, and gone was don Daniel. Gone too was my world with everything and everyone I had known. Gone was I, and cut off I would remain from all things familiar until the rain dies on the shining faces of the hours as they lift to savor the freedom of the cycle broken.

Well, I was here for a reason and the purpose of it all would shortly be made manifest. I felt it in my bones. Even now, if don Daniel was correct, someone was awaiting me at the exit from the cave. I went to the far end of the chamber, to the edge of the abyss. The log bridge was there as promised. It was nothing more than a tree trunk spanning the chasm, however. I hated the idea of walking across it, and I decided to cross by straddling it and pulling myself forward with my hands and forearms.

As I reached the other side, a blackness enveloped me just after I saw the ladder descending down the side of the bottomless pit. Over my shoulder I had my wand in its case, in which a few pieces of flint were preserved. I could light a fire but there would be no way to descend and carry the light. I would have to descend in complete darkness. In a curious way the symbolism was appropriate. I told myself to have faith and go into the inkiness of ignorance to emerge in a new light of revelation on the other side. Grabbing the ladder firmly, I slid myself over the ledge and descended slowly. One step at a time . . . it seemed to take forever. The ladder itself twisted in my hands and entangled between my feet like some living thing; the pit felt like some petrified intestine of a long extinct prehistoric beast.

At last I reached the tunnel opening. Climbing in and groping my way forward, keeping my left hand in contact with the wall of the tunnel, I made slow progress. Soon I felt a vibration in the stone which I quickly recognized as the distant booming of drums, and then I could barely hear the music of flutes and conch shells. Best of all, as I rounded a bend, in the distance I saw light.

> *Aztec pendulums and abandoned hoot owls*
> *inhabit a corner of my mind*
> *where clockwork galaxies derail unscheduled time frames*
> *and electric arches drill the ashes of Antarctica*
> *into a foxless Mexican sky.*

Reaching the end of the tunnel, I stood on a stone-faced ledge overlooking a valley open to the big sky and dominated by a pyramid—the moon pyramid that don Daniel spoke of. At first sight it was exotic, marvelous, splendorous, and barbaric. I remembered a line from Lao Tzu's *Way of Life*: "from wonder into wonder, existence opens."

Fig. 3.2. "At first sight it was exotic, marvelous, splendorous, and barbaric."

The pyramid was constructed of translucent white alabaster. As I would learn later, the site itself was laid out as a rectangle about 380 by 330 yards. The complex was surrounded by a stone wall decorated with painted seashells. Three broad avenues led to and converged upon this enclosure, where they ended in fortified gates at the wall of shells. The central gate was sculpted in a rich baroque motif and was surmounted by the carved figure of Tecciztécatl, the moon god. Beyond this gate stood a court for the ritual ball game, which in turn was surrounded by lesser buildings, including store rooms, priest's quarters, and rooms for fasting and penance. The pyramid measured 120 yards by 90 yards at its base, not including the platform on which it stood. It rose in five tiers to a height of 90 feet, and the face angle of the first slope was 43.35 degrees. On the south side was a staircase 15 yards wide, flanked by balustrades in the form of huge snakes whose open mouths ended at the foot of the staircase. These balustrades were painted blue, black, and white. Toward the upper end of the staircase, they changed inclination and became almost vertical, each topped with two platforms. A figure of a stone rabbit, used as a standard-bearer, was seated on each platform. From the back of each rabbit rose a banner plume made of feathers.

The top of the pyramid was leveled to form a terrace on which stood the twin temples of the two moon goddesses, Metztli and Coyolxauhqui. The main body of each temple was a boxlike structure with no windows and only a single door. Each temple was surmounted by high, sloping roofs in the shape of truncated pyramids made of wood and faced with stucco. The lower part of each roof was decorated and painted in alternate vertical stripes of blue, black, and white. The tops of the roofs were crested and shaped in the form of seashells and copper bells.

On the terrace outside the temples stood two stone blocks covered with hieroglyphs on which men were sometimes sacrificed. Beside these altars burned great braziers as tall as a man. The other temples and courtyards were filled with sculptures and the walls of the buildings were adorned with frescoes and bas-reliefs.

Priests on top of the pyramid were dancing, chanting, playing drums, gongs, flutes, whistles, and conch shells. The courtyards, plaza, and avenues were packed with dancing people. Painted, adorned, bejeweled, they moved in sensuous serpentine rhythm. They were dressed in loincloths, embroidered cloaks, and feathered headdresses. This was New Year's Day. The celebration of the Festival of the Stopping of the Waters, dedicated to Tlaloc, the rain god and Chalchiuhtlicue, Goddess of Terrestrial Waters. In the Nahuatl tongue this festival is called Atlcaualo or Quauitleua.

I stood on the ledge looking down on the scene and was filled with a rush of enormous pleasure verging on poetic ecstasy . . .

Aloneness flows. A chill, dry wine on the tongue. Even time, the inseparable companion, will not follow here. One is left unchaperoned to explore this island of hours and miles that spreads to infinity in glowing darkness. The soft, red earth caresses the feet and strokes between the toes like a lover's fingers bent upon the ancient quest. Now, in this place, living is real and whole. Forever burns with a white shouting flame, searching unquenchably through luminous eons of grass.

I heard a sound to my left and turned just in time to see an Indian climbing onto the ledge from the trail below. I was immediately struck by his resemblance to don Daniel, only he looked much younger. He was dressed simply in a cotton loincloth and plain cloak. He wore a headpiece of small, polished obsidian mirrors and yellow feathers. He was about 5'4" in height and had a barrel chest and short legs. His black hair was shoulder length and he had clear black eyes and a large hooked nose. He greeted me in a musical Nahuatl, the tongue of the Aztecs, a language in which I was fluent, and even allowing for the changes that occur in language idioms over five hundred years, I knew that in a short time I would be comfortable with the language here too.

"You are the awaited one," he said. "My name is Ballcourt Smoke and I am your guide. How are you called?"

"Mark," I replied.

"Here, dress yourself," he said, handing me a loincloth, cloak, feathered headdress, and leather sandals. He helped me put on the loincloth, which went around the waist and between the legs and was knotted so that one end hung down in front and the other behind. The rectangular cloak was of rich cotton worked exquisitely with metallic-colored hummingbird feathers in the form of a wind-jewel—a symbol of Quetzalcoatl. It wound around the body under the left armpit and then knotted over the right shoulder. The headdress was of green feathers and the sandals had straps that wound around the leg from the ankle to the knee.

"Where to?" I asked.

"Look," he said, pointing below. "Do you see the ball court? That first building to the left is the palace of Jade Eagle, master of the red and black, keeper of the sacred count of days, and high priest of the moon. He is waiting for us and will answer all your questions."

In about twenty minutes we had reached the valley and were standing outside the palace. It stood on a platform about 15 feet high and its stone walls were covered with lime. It was a self-contained, inward-looking complex. The walls facing the street were blank. We were admitted, and as we entered, I saw that all the principal rooms opened onto interior courtyards. The floor was of white stucco and the roof was supported by elaborately carved wooden pillars resting on stone blocks.

Ballcourt Smoke took me on a tour of the premises, which included an anteroom, an audience chamber, dining and reception rooms, separate quarters for men and women, store rooms, a kitchen, and a servant's hall. The palace itself was surrounded by a walled garden. Awnings of dyed cotton cloth shaded the patios, and the doorways were closed by curtains sewn with silver bells. We then went to the dining room, where we feasted on wild boar, turkey, fish with green chile and tomatoes, tortillas, and chocolate.

After the meal Ballcourt Smoke took me to the audience chamber where I met Jade Eagle for the first time. He was seated on an *icpalli*, a kind of legless chair made of wickerwork with the base resting directly on the floor and the backrest reaching higher than his head. I followed Ballcourt Smoke's lead and sat down cross-legged on a woven mat at Jade Eagle's feet.

"Welcome, Mark, my son. I know you must have many questions and I will try to answer them all, but first let us smoke."

He pulled out an ornate pipe made of silver and tortoiseshell and filled it with a rich mixture of tobacco, marijuana, powdered charcoal, flowers, pulverized amber, bitumen, and other aromatic substances. We passed the pipe back and forth. Jade Eagle and Ballcourt Smoke would pinch their nostrils as they began to inhale, so I did the same. The smoke was savory and pungent, not at all harsh, and in a few moments I was feeling very good indeed.

Jade Eagle spoke: "Mark, my son, there is much to tell and not much time to tell it. As you know, we are able to see clearly into the future, the days that are to come, and we can communicate with our descendants in those far distant times. We know that the end of this next fifty-two-year cycle will see the arrival of the pale ones and the fall and total destruction of our culture. This is ordained, this must be, and we are reconciled to it. It will be the passing away of this cycle of time, which is under the influence of our Lord Tezcatlipoca, Smoking Mirror. The next cycle of time, in which the pale ones rule, will be under the influence of our Lord Quetzalcoatl, Feathered Serpent. In your day it is believed that the cycles of time dominated by Tezcatlipoca were all evil, and those cycles under the influence of Quetzalcoatl were all good and benevolent. This is not so, and I shall explain why presently. What neither you nor the people of your time know, and this is of supreme importance, is the date for the end of the Quetzalcoatl cycle. The cycle begins with the arrival of the man called Cortés in the year of your calendar 1519, and will last 468 years. This means that the end of that time cycle will occur in your year 1987.*

"These cycles of time are the ways of fate, natural events not to be regretted. I must now explain to you the true meaning of the name Quetzalcoatl. The outward meaning is the one generally known, 'feathered serpent.' The inner meaning, known only to the initiated brothers of the priesthood, is 'precious twin.' This refers to his nature as the planetary god of Venus in his dual aspects of morning and evening star. Of these two, the morning star is the Quetzal, or precious one. In his other aspect as the evening star, he is the evil one, Xolotl, the animal, the dispenser of ill fortune. He is a monstrosity with backward-turned feet. It is this aspect that rules the cycle of Quetzalcoatl that runs from your years 1519 to 1987. It is a period of evil magic during which humankind becomes inhuman; a time of fierce beasts, general misfortune, and increasing viciousness. During this cycle nothing can be made of life and nothing will remain. People will be incapable in all the things of the earth. They will become like wanderers driven by the wind. In all things failures. They wish to be important, but in the end they become simply nothing. This cycle also ends the Period of the Fourth Sun.

"Let me explain the Suns and the forces that rule them. First there was the Fire Sun, when all things ended in fire. Then there was the Wind Sun, when all things were destroyed by storms and hurricanes. Next came the Water Sun, which ended in the Great Flood. This present sun is the fourth creation. It is in effect the Earth Sun of Movement and will finally close in 2012 with great earthquakes. The period from 1987 to 2012 will be one of increasing calamity. In all this can be seen a grand mandala of time. At the completion of the Fourth Sun, a terrible earthquake will tear down all human structures and destroy most or all of humanity. Beyond

---

* This date was calculated by Tony Shearer in his books *Quetzalcoatl, Lord of the Dawn* (Healdsburg, Calif.: Naturegraph, 1971) and *Beneath the Moon and Under the Sun* (Albuquerque, N.M.: Sun Publishing,1975). —*JMJ*

this we cannot see. No one knows for certain whether the end to come will be a final destruction or whether a Fifth Age will develop. Yet we who are your friends hope for the best. We look upon the last Quetzalcoatl cycle as a time of fertilization, when manure for a garden is spread upon the earth, from which will spring the beautiful flowers of a Fifth Age or Sun. For this hope and reason you are here now, to receive a solid knowledge of the wisdom of the Ancients—wise sages ancient even to us. This knowledge can be found in the sacred book called the Pyramid of Fire. A copy of the drawings in this sacred book, and readings from it, were given to you in your own time by don Daniel. Here, if you are willing, you will be initiated into its secret esoteric meaning so that you can pass it on or carry it forward yourself into the new age if there be one. What you must know is that there are men here in this time and place who do not want this knowledge passed on. They are men who work with the powers of darkness, who do not wish for the continuation of life in a new Fifth Age. They are powerful men—intelligent, crafty, and masters of black magic. They will stop at nothing to prevent you from gaining initiation and carrying this wisdom forward, and they know you are here now. For this reason time is short."

"But, Jade Eagle," I interrupted, "if you initiate me here and now, how can they stop us?"

"If it were only that simple, Mark, my son, there would be no problem. You see, there are thirteen pages to the sacred codex. For each page you must be initiated by a different master, and each master lives in a different location at his own temple. I myself will give you the first page freely, for it describes the origin and structure of the universe and can be understood easily with a little meditation. But for the others you must travel to each location that is appropriate to the teaching in each page and receive instruction from the masters firsthand. This is cosmic law. Nothing this valuable can be obtained so easily. Only through knowledge, reflection, effort, sacrifice, and love can you overcome the obstacles and achieve your goal. Will you undertake this task?"

"Yes I will," I replied.

"Good. Then this is what we shall do. Shortly I will show you how to read the pictures on the first page. Then tomorrow you will leave for the east, to the Land of the Rubber People on the coast, to see my friend Obsidian Headwall, who will interpret the second page for you and give you further instructions. I will send Ballcourt Smoke with you as a guide, companion, and interpreter. If all goes well, he will stay with you to the completion of your task. You must leave tomorrow because we do not know what our enemies plan or what they intend to do. Also, tomorrow is an auspicious day for the start of a journey. Our enemies don't know our plans and if we move quickly, we may catch them off guard and evade further detection. I believe this palace is being watched, but if you mingle with the celebrating crowds in the morning, I am sure you can slip away unseen. Now, Ballcourt Smoke, go and gather what is necessary for the trip from my store rooms."

"I am on my way," he said, and left us.

Jade Eagle did not speak for some time. He then got up and went to a wooden chest against the far wall and removed a deerskin parchment painted in brilliant colors. It was the first page of the Pyramid of Fire.

He placed it in front of me and said, "The reason why the men of your day cannot interpret the hieroglyphs and picture writings is that they do not understand how they function. Even if they did, there is almost no one left who knows the oral traditions. You see, the pictographs are part of an oral tradition and are in reality based upon a system of mnemonics, aids to the memory. The initiated brother looks at each symbol and character and notes its positional relationship to the others, and this triggers his memory of the true esoteric meaning of the glyphs. This book, the Pyramid of Fire, contains encapsulated in short form our knowledge of the universe, its function, and man's relationship to it; systems of astrology and yoga; events of the end times; the meaning of sacrifice; and the paths to enlightenment. Now listen carefully . . ."

Jade Eagle stood at my shoulder, pointed at the picture-glyphs and interpreted them in the following manner:

[Read pages 1 and 2 of the codex, found in chapter 4 on pages 65–67. —JMJ]

The reading was intensive. "Now it is time to rest," said Jade Eagle, "for the journey is long and hazardous. If you manage to overcome the obstacles and succeed in realizing each of the pages, we shall meet here again, coming full circle for the final initiation. Good luck to you, and may Tonatiuh, our Lord the Sun, keep you safe."

At the break of dawn Ballcourt Smoke and I mingled with the crowds of revelers and made our way easily past the eastern gate and out onto the trail. We were off to the shore of the True Cross and the rising sun at New Year. What a grand adventure! A vast panorama spread out before us. In the dreamtime of the quest we passed waterfalls of pearls, fangs, and arrows splashing in sun-drenched pools. This is the dream that comes crawling forth from the lizard tyrant's bed, to trail the bloodless comet's tail in a thousand buzzing ways and spill open upon a blue beach with no tongue. To heart speak in your own cloud emptied of fishes and pass through the narrow reef of time where armless Olmecs with no moss dance, where three chance to play on the beach of creation, and where I heard stone growing in a cliff.

Part 3

And as three forces create everything in all which is made,
there are four states of matter and four deities that govern them.

PYRAMID OF FIRE, 4:10–11

Burning water in a parrot green sky, a magician's tower moldering over an afternoon of golden dwarfs and hourglass highs. Show me how to measure the falcon's frozen flight, the meadow's obsidian cry, my own deaf shadow shouldering the wind, or show me the dream's shore instantly obeyed, boxed to fit the mathematics of an insect's eye.

On the fourth day after leaving Jade Eagle's palace, Ballcourt Smoke pulled me off the trail and we hid behind a boulder. We watched silently as a band of twenty warriors trotted two abreast in a line, moving past our vantage point. They were coming from behind us and heading toward the coast of the True Cross, just as we were. They wore the battle dress of Jaguar Knights—tightly fitting cat skins that covered their bodies, arms, and legs, and were pulled up over their heads so that their faces showed through the animal's open jaws. Their shields bore the glyph for the date 3 Cipactli (3 Crocodile).

"Trouble," said Ballcourt Smoke. "I don't think they're looking for us now, but they are probably responding to word of our coming, and shortly all the roads will be watched. They're in the employ of 3 Crocodile—no one knows his other name, but he is pure evil, one of the vilest and most potent sorcerers of our time. He runs a school of black magic near Lake Catemaco that is famous throughout the empire. He is greatly feared and is left strictly alone. He pays no tribute to Tenochtitlan. He is also the absolute ruler of a fortified city-state called Cipactlan, near the lake where the school is located."

"How long will we be safe on the road?" I asked.

"For a little while, but not much longer. I know this region well, and in any case I have many friends and relatives in this area. We will go now to a safe house and make further plans. I think that shortly we will have to take to the rivers, but for now we will stay on the trail."

We moved on warily. The wind's antlered tongue dusted my ears with mossy forests and unzipped the music of flowers. I watched two hawks do a mating dance across the sky.

"Look at those birds," exclaimed Ballcourt Smoke, "The omen is plain to see!"

"How do you read it?" I asked, puzzled.

"Danger at a distance, trouble from the left. We must pick up the pace."

And so the text ends after Marty (a.k.a. Mark/Marco) is given the first page* and embarks on a journey to receive the initiatory lesson/meaning of the next page. The whole underworld journey, accessed through the famous Cerro Rabon in Mazatec country that is indeed crisscrossed with deep caves, takes place five hundred years ago and is a metaphor for the

---

* There is some ambiguity as to whether or not the first two pages were at one time considered one page in Marty's thinking. The content of the pages seems of a piece, though they existed as separate pages in the copy of the text sent to me in 1995. Here in the novella they are considered to be "the first page." (The manuscript of the novella was labeled "11/14/1995, rough draft.") Was the codex actually twelve or thirteen pages? In most instances it seems there are thirteen.

thirteen-step program of initiation into *ekpyrosis,* ascension at death and the end of time.

In his novella Marty draws heavily from the text of the Pyramid of Fire, but we also find chants and prayers that may come from actual ceremonies with don Daniel. Some of the flowery prose is clearly adapted from Marty's poems from his collection *Time Waits;* these admirable lines provide alternative, embellished, versions of those poems. Marty began working on this novella in 1995, after we began discussing publishing options for his work.

It is likely that some of the events in this story did occur: the trip to caves in Cerro Rabon, the mushroom ceremony. And who is to say that some of the inner visionary states recounted in the story were not glimpsed by Marty? Stranger experiences have been reported. Regardless of whether the story is taken as absolute truth, it does illustrate some important features of the Pyramid of Fire and the character of don Daniel, as well as Marty's relationship to both.

Regarding the time scheme in the novella, the year 1467 was fifty-two years before 1519, which, according to the work of Tony Shearer, initiated the countdown to 1987, a journey of nine "hell realm" periods of fifty-two years each. The thirteen stages of the initiatory journey of the Pyramid of Fire do not, strictly speaking, correspond to fifty-two-year periods. Marty echoes a popular conception that ties 1987 into the Mayan Long Count end date of 2012 by generalizing the end-time's dynamic into a twenty-six-year countdown.*

Without trying to guess the details of Marty's unfinished novella, we can at least summarize each page concisely and thereby divine the lesson or teaching of each page, which would have defined the story that Marty wanted to tell:

Page 1   Creation and the Celestial Hierarchy

Page 2   Harmony of the Spheres; "As above, so below"; and the Limited Vision of Man

Page 3   The Trinity Principle and the Domains of the Universe

---

* This is perfectly appropriate for a fictional allegory, but the actual relationship between the Nahuatl/Toltec end-date and the Maya end-date is more complicated. See chapters 6, 7, and 12 in my book *Maya Cosmogenesis 2012* (Rochester, Vt.: Bear and Company, 1998).

Finally, we can do the same for page 13 and even guess what the final events in the novella would have been, for they would involve the sacrifice at the end of mortal life paralleled to the New Fire sacrifice:

A very significant and profound metaphysical teaching is presented here: the end of time is equated with the visionary ascent, the mystic initiation. It is this insight that defines this book's subtitle: *Spiritual Ascent at the End of Time.* We have a clue in the novella that after completing his initiations, Mark would return to the palace of Jade Eagle for the final initiation, corresponding to the thirteenth page. This would result in the ultimate self-sacrifice that is the ritual death attending the mystic initiation into divine life. Thus, we may imagine the final section of Marty's story to be about his (or his protagonist's) ascent of the stairs of the "pyramid of fire" (the Hill of the Star in the New Fire ceremony). At the top the fire priests await his willing sacrifice of his ego in order to merge with Quetzalcoatl, which according to my reconstruction of the New Fire ceremony represents the Pleiades in the zenith with sun at nadir.[3] The axis runs from the nadir sun (in November = in Scorpio) through the ascending stairs of the pyramid to the Pleiades in Taurus (as the highest center of consciousness) in the zenith. This is a Kundalini chakra axis, otherwise known as the Evolutionary Axis. With this ascension axis activated, the door of deity is opened and it only takes a consciously willing sacrifice of self in order to merge. The metaphysical meaning of this ceremony is central to the Vedic soma rite and is discussed by Ananda Coomaraswamy in his discussion of "self-naughting."[4]

The New Fire ritual is largely regarded as a literal heart sacrifice, but as the text of the Pyramid of Fire will reveal, this literal practice was a late degradation of the original spiritual meaning (which probably came from Toltec teachings). The dissolution of the ego-self, to be reabsorbed back into the solar light of Tonatiuh, is what Mark would have to experience on a visionary or spiritual level. We can only guess as to how Marty would have painted this picture.* We will discuss this in greater detail when we look more closely at the last page of the codex in chapter 6.

Many of the diagrams accompanying the codex in the following chapter were located by Marty in the known codices and were added to the text he sent me in 1995. I have located others, primarily images of individual deities, based upon names and descriptions in the text. Repeated readings and a meditative state of mind are most helpful in deepening your understanding of the perennial principles this sacred text encodes. As you read, imagine the words being read aloud or performed—as in a dramaturgical performance. Be open to the secret whispers of things not visible to the eye that is focused upon only surface appearances. And remember, as it says in another great work of poetic wisdom tradition:

> *Knowledge cannot stay concealed,*
> *Hidden in some secret burrow;*
> *Words of wisdom never vanish,*
> *Though the wise men pass away.*[5]

---

* This may have been very much like the mystic initiation that I describe for the initiatory center of Izapa in chapter 23 of my book *Maya Cosmogenesis 2012.*

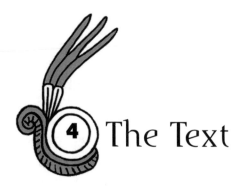

(4) The Text

We are now nearly ready to read the text. But before we begin it is essential to develop some facility with Nahuatl pronunciation. This is easier than the forbidding look of the words might suggest.

The consonant combinations *tz* and *tl* are perhaps the most difficult to master. The *tz* sounds more like *dz*. The *tl* is softly exploded off the tip of the tongue. If it occurs at the end of a word, as in *Nahuatl*, it sounds the same as in *bottle*. Practice this sound slowly at first, and then more quickly. Vowels are almost always sounded as in Spanish usage, which follows consistent rules of pronunciation: *a* as in *father, e* as in *way, i* as in *feet, o* as in *toe, u* as in *too*. The letter *c* is hard unless it comes before *i*. For *cc*, the first *c* is hard, the second *c* sounds like an *s*. For example: Tecciztécatl = Tek-seez-tay-cottle.

Syllables with accent marks are emphasized. In the absence of an accent mark somewhere in a word, emphasis falls on the next to last syllable. If no accent mark is found, which is rare, there is no emphasis on any particular syllable and the word is pronounced with uniform emphasis throughout.[1] The suffixes *-atl* and *-otl* at the end of names refer to gender, male and female respectively, with *-atl* rhyming with *bottle* and *-otl* pronounced as in *boatle*.

Perhaps in the future an audio recording of Nahuatl will be available. See appendix 2 for more phonetic spellings of Nahuatl words.

As for the physical appearance of the Pyramid of Fire, I have modified many of the line breaks (the transcription I received was written in paragraph form) and have implemented a system of line numbering for ease of reference in discussion of the text: 3:2–6 refers to Pyramid of Fire page 3, lines 2 through 6.

Throughout the codex deity names appear in bold upon first use and their functions, qualities, and/or areas of governance are italicized. In rare instances I have added a comma, exchanged a colon for a comma, or added a clarifying adverb for easier reading.

According to Marty, during his various moves the thirteenth page of the codex and the drawings he made were lost. The drawings were never found, but fortunately, after resurfacing in 2000, Marty had a friend of his send me a tape of one of his earliest readings of the codex. Originally recorded on a wire recorder in the early 1960s, the sound quality was fairly good but faint. After boosting the signal, I was able to transcribe the lost thirteenth page and then read my transcription to Marty over the phone for confirmation.

The footnotes include a minimum number of relevant comments referenced to the text of the codex in this chapter, but more in-depth commentary can be found in chapter 5.

Pyramid of Fire
(Codex Matz-Ayauhtla)

[Page 1]

1   Over all, in all worlds and in all times exists
    Tloque Nahuaque, Lord of the Intimate Vicinity,
    universal spirit, unimaginable, without form
    the Absolute.

5   From within him is born **Tonacatecuhtli,**
    Lord of Our Sustainment, *Father of all* the gods
    and all the worlds, *Creator of all* the cosmoses
    and all the galaxies.

9   From within him are born **Tzitzímime,**
    giants that descend from the sky above our galaxy,
    the Milky Way.

12 From within him is born **Tonatiuh,** *the Sun,*
    Lord of our Solar System, giver of life to all planets,
    plants, beasts, and men.

15 From within him are born his sons
    and his daughters that revolve reverently around him,
    the planets:
    Mixcóatl, the Cloud Serpent, Saturn;
    Tezcatlipoca, the Smoking Mirror, Jupiter;
    Huitzilopochtli, the Hummingbird Magician, Mars;
    Itzpapálotl, the Obsidian Butterfly, Venus;
    Paynal, the Speedy Runner, Mercury;

Tlaltecuhtli, Lord of Our Planet, *the Earth*, living
sphere of earth, rock, air, and want.

25   Over which reigns **Xochiquetzal,** Flourished Plume,
Nature, goddess of all that lives, grows, flowers,
and is engendered.

28   And from the Earth and Nature is born
Metztli, the last, the end, *the Moon*.

[Page 2]

1   These eight levels of divinity, each one of which is nothing
for him from whom they issue forth
and infinite for him to whom it gives life,
resemble the eight notes of the cosmic musical scale:

5   Tonatiuh, Mixcóatl, Tezcatlipoca, Paynal, and Metztli,*

6   as the Sun, the planets, and the Moon,
sound the eight notes of the solar musical scale.

8   The eight notes of the music of nature
sound as heroes, men, animals, insects, plants,
soil, rock, and metals.

11   The eight notes of human music
sound as spirit, heart, head, semen, blood,
viscera, nerves, and bone.

14   Because that which is above created that which is below
and that which is low reflects that which is high,
the Universe is Tezcatlipoca, Smoking Mirror,
in which man still does not see clearly.

---

* To complete the sun, moon, and planets, this list should also include Huitzilopochtli, Itzpapálotl, and Tlaltecuhtli. Marty told me, however, that the list was given to him without these three included.

[Page 3]

1   All things of Heaven and Earth are created by three forces
     without which nothing can be
     produced, made manifest, or developed.
     That is why each of the worlds is not governed by one god
     but by three:
     one masculine, one feminine, and one mediator;
     one active, one passive, one impartial.

8   Only Tloque Nahuaque is *One.*

9   Tonacatecuhtli, Father of Our Sustainment,
     and **Tonacacíhuatl,** Lady of Our Sustainment,
     united by Ometecuhtli, Lord of Duality,
     govern *all the galaxies.*

13   **Centzonhuitznáuac,** four hundred to the south
     and **Centzon Mimixcoa,** four hundred to the north,
     reconciled by Tzitzímime, giants that descend from above,
     govern the *Milky Way.*

17   Only Tonatiuh is one, the *Sun.*

18   Tlaltecuhtli, Lord of the Earth,
     and **Tlazoltécoatl,*** Mother Earth,
     reconciled by **Coatlicue,** dressed with serpents,
     govern *our planet.*

---

* The name appears as Tlazoltéotl in the text and is pronounced as Tlazoltécoatl on the
recording. Both names, however, refer to the same deity.

22   Xochiquetzal, Flourished Plume,
      Xochipilli, Flourished Prince,
      and their son **Centéotl,** God of Corn,
      govern *nature.*

26   Metztli and her sister **Coyolxauhqui,**
      painted with jingle bells and craters,
      Tecciztécatl, He of the Marine Conch,
      govern the *Moon.*

30   **Mictlantecuhtli,** Lord of Death,
      and **Mictecacíhuatl,** Lady of Death,
      reconciled by **Teoyaomiqui,** Lord of the Dead Warrior,
      govern the worlds of *Hell.*

[Page 4]

1   Each world is the play of three gods,
     three forces and their field of action.
     As one or another god guides, as one or another god follows,
     as one or another god concludes,
     there can be gotten six classes of games,
     six processes that create all that occurs or may occur.
     These six classes of divine games decide the growth,
     the decadence, the purification, the infirmity, the curation,
     and the regeneration of the world.

10   And as three forces create everything in all which is made,
     there are four states of matter and four deities that govern them:

     Xiuhtecuhtli, Lord of the Year,
     governs active masculine matter, *fire.*
     Chalchiuhtlicue, She of the Jeweled Gown,
     governs passive, feminine matter, *water.*
     Ehécatl, God of the Wind,
     governs impartial unifying mediating matter, *wind.*
     Cihuacóatl, the Woman Serpent,
     governs matter that is inert, current of all forces, *earth.*

20   As three forces create everything, there are four states of time,
     four seasons of the year, and four deities govern them:

22   **Xipe Totec,** the Skinned One, governs the ardent season
     when the earth becomes naked, *spring.*

24 **Tláloc,** He Who Makes Germination, governs the humid
season when the earth enrobes, *summer.*

26 **Chicomecoatl,** the Seventh Serpent, Goddess of Corn,
governs the windy season when the earth adorns herself, *autumn.*

28 **Itzlacoliuhqui,** Spiraled Knife, governs the barren season
when the earth grows cold, *winter.*

Fig. 4.1. The gods of Life and Death

[Page 5]

1   Man does not will when he wars, loves, and reaps;
     it is the rhythms of the great gods, the planets,
     that act over him and make him do.
     When man comprehends that by himself he can do nothing,
     then he can learn to serve the gods; so,
     he must become conscious of the rhythms of the gods.

7   The calendar that governs the life of man, the Tonalpohualli,
     is based on the rites of the planets that turn closest to the Earth:
     Paynal, Mercury;
     Quetzalcóatl, Venus;
     and Huitzilopochtli, Mars.

12   It is Paynal who governs the movement and the dance of men.
     Quetzalcóatl governs their growing and their fertility.
     Huitzilopochtli governs the fight and the war of men.

15   And as the sun lights the Earth in the same form every 365 days,
     every 117 days Paynal shines over the earth in the same form,
     every 585 days shines Quetzalcóatl in the same form,
     every 780 days shines Huitzilopochtli in the same form.

19   So the week has 13 days,
     factor of the cycles of Paynal and Quetzalcóatl.
     The month has 20 days, factor of the cycle of Huitzilopochtli.

22   And the Tonalpohualli, this Holy Year of the Planets,
     has 13 times 20 or 260 days.

24   And parallel to this Holy Year of the Planets
     occurs the Year of the Sun
     by which man plants, reaps, and recognizes the stations.

27   And the two years represent the double play
     of divinity in the heavens,
     one the Play of the Divine Many
     and the other the Play of the Divine One.

31   So one Tonalpohualli measures $2^{1}/_{4}$ cycles of Paynal.
     One Tonalpohualli measures $^{4}/_{9}$ of a cycle of Quetzalcóatl.
     One Tonalpohualli measures $^{1}/_{3}$ of a cycle of Huitzilopochtli.
     One Tonalpohualli measures $^{2}/_{3}$ of a cycle of Mixcóatl.
     The Tonalpohualli measures the cycles of all the planets.

36   After 9 Tonalpohualli, Paynal, Quetzalcóatl,
     and Huitzilopochtli all shine over the Earth in the same form;
     everything begins again.
     A new opportunity is given.

40 After 73 Tonalpohualli (52 solar years), this Holy Year of
the Planets coincides with the year of Tonatiuh, the Sun.
During five days all fires are put out and a new fire is lit
at the sacred mountain, a fire taken directly from the solar source.
And with great ceremony all fires are lit again
from this one Son of the Sun.

46 After 108 Tonalpohualli, the rhythms of the minor planets unite
with the rhythms of the greater planets;
all the planets that give form and character to man
shine together in the same form.
Such is the duration of the life of man.

51 After 657* Tonalpohualli (468 solar years), the cycles
of the minor planets and the cycles of the Sun end together.
Tonatiuh, Quetzalcóatl, Huitzilopochtli, and Paynal
shine again at the same time in the same form.
This is an Age, the duration of the life of a culture.

---

* While Marty's original text states this as 767 Tonalpohualli, it is 657 Tonalpohualli on the
recording—and, given the context, 657 is mathematically correct.

[Page 6]

1   In the heavens over the Earth sails Tecciztécatl,
He of the Marine Conch (the Moon), and Tonatiuh, the Sun.
The Earth and all its creatures are under their power.

4   On the Earth exists the worlds of nature:
the informal life of waters, trees, insects, animals,
and two classes of men.
One class is the ordinary man, naked, inert, always menaced
by death's darts.
The other class is the superior man.
In the shade of the altar
the maguey spines of penance become for him
the wings of the soul
and in his hands he harmonizes the four states of matter.
He has achieved consciousness.
He has achieved the power of Truth and can act.
He is!

17   The other man is like an agonized animal
tied to the tree from which he eats.
He gives his vital energy to Tecciztécatl, the Moon,
while his body is eaten by Tlaltecuhtli, the Earth.
So everything devours and is devoured, eats and is eaten
in the cosmic hierarchy.
Plants eat from minerals and are eaten by animals.
The animals eat plants and in their turn are eaten by the Earth.
So does man, as animal organism, devour plants
and is devoured by Earth in due time.

27   And if he is only body, he has no other destiny.
But the superior man feeds on sacrifice; he develops his soul
and his soul becomes food for Tonatiuh, the Sun.
So, as the maguey spines rest on the straw bed,
the soul of the liberated man rests on the Hill of Heaven.

*Fig. 4.2. Tlazolteotl and the Falcon Herald of the Gods,
from Codex Borbonicus*

[Page 7]

1   Man is born through Tlazoltéotl, the Mother Earth,
in her Ixcuina disguise as Consumer of Waste,
as she who takes into herself everything that dies
and putrefies it and re-creates it, renewing herself incessantly
and renewing all that grows upon her.
She carries her dead skin while a new one grows underneath.

7   Over near the entrance to the Kingdom of Matter
is the germ or symbol of the man to be born.
He emerges from the Mother Earth into the world of men,
but Tezcatlipoca, the Falcon Herald of the Gods, is also there.

Over his head is the symbol of the Milky Way,
over his chest is the solar disk, and in his hands are the wings
of the soul of man, the offering of the gods at birth.

14   And between the Mother Earth and the Herald of Heaven
is found the symbol of the dual nature of man:
the earthly centipede of his spinal column interlaced
with the celestial serpent of consciousness that can inhabit him.

18   And again, under to the left, we see that which remains
when the wings of the serpent have flown:
the heart of the dead warrior, his head over the altar,
and the skull of the dead prisoner on the cranium stake,
because life will return to its source
and the soul will return to its beginning.

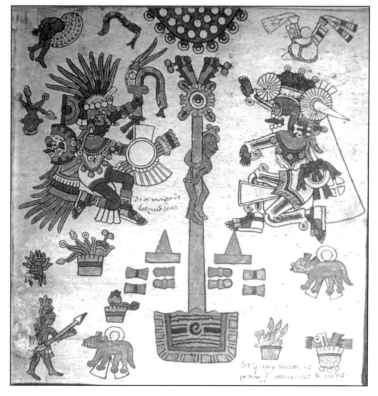

Fig. 4.3. "And over all, the Milky Way of innumerable suns"

[Page 8]

1   Man climbs the tree of life between Tonatiuh, the Sun,
and Mictlantecuhtli, Lord of the Hells and of Death.
At the foot of the tree that grows between the symbols
that represent earth, air, water, and fire,
the constituent parts that intervened in his conception
are reunited: the semen with which his parents engendered him,
the pig of personality, the eagle of spirit,
and in a basket spotted with stars, the bones of mortality
and the wings of the soul.

10   The summit of the tree is Death where shines the Sun itself,
the Midnight Sun from which radiate the four paths or ways.
From here surge the wings of the soul finally liberated,
while above, each of his various parts, separated by death,
runs to its destiny.

15   To the left, to the fields of Death, goes the corpse draped in flesh,
the beast that returns to the root of the tree.
To the right, to the side of Life, goes the serpent of consciousness
that came from the Sun and to the Sun returns,
the spirit by which man is transfigured in the stellar world.
And over all, the Milky Way of innumerable suns.

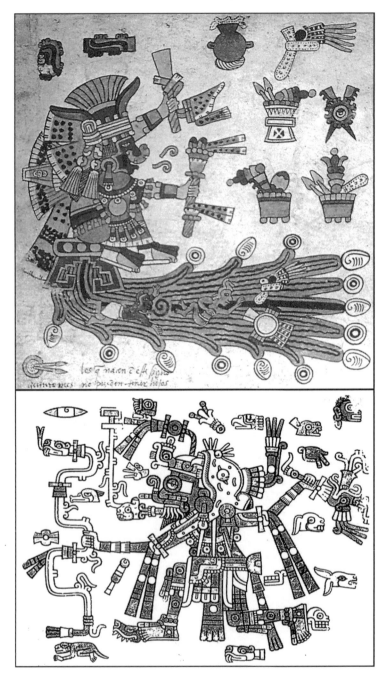

Fig. 4.4. Chalchiuhtlicue (top) and Tláloc

[Page 9]

1   Chalchiuhtlicue, Goddess of Terrestrial Waters,
of that which flows, runs, surges, forward and *down*,
arriving always at profounder levels.
Chalchiuhtlicue swells the fruits and flowers
only so that they may *drop*.
Chalchiuhtlicue fills the gourd of pulque so that man may *forget*.
Chalchiuhtlicue, current that *descends* in the course of rivers,
current that flows in the course of time,
making men's wastes and the implements of war inert
and taking them to their inevitable end.

11   Tláloc, God of Celestial Water, god of the vapor that *rises*
from the earth warmed by the sun after the rains,
god of the mist that *ascends* from the valleys at dawn,
god of the water that returns to its source in the clouds that swim
over the highest peaks, god of the humid incense from which rise
the copal prayers and the prayers of sacrifice.

17   Tláloc is the return of vapor that strains to rise,
is the return of time that strains to *remember*.
Tláloc, God of the Fight Against the Current,
with whose aid the hero battles against the torrent
toward his own origin and beginning,
toward the wings of his soul,
the wings that Tláloc hides in the hero's past.

[Page 10]*

1   Quetzalcóatl, the Plumed Serpent, moves between gods and men,
because Quetzalcóatl is God who permeates man
and is the man that achieves God.
The Plumed Serpent is born when that which slithers over the
Earth
grows wings to be elevated to Heaven.

6   Quetzalcóatl is a superior man, the inner circle of humanity,
the link between gods and men.

8   All men *are made of* earth, air, water, and fire,
creatures of Cihuacóatl, Chalchiuhtlicue, Ehécatl, and
Xiuhtecuhtli.
All men *receive their forms* from the planets by Mixcóatl,
Tezcatlipoca, Huitzilopochtli, Itzpapálotl, Paynal, and Metztli.
But in their hearts and in their semen, each man *has his own* coatl,
his own serpent, the energy of Tonatiuh, the power of the Sun
itself.
And in this serpent sleeps consciousness, in this serpent
is hidden his divinity. From this serpent his wings will grow.

16   In the ordinary man the serpent has but one head—hurting and
cruel,
and lacking control of the energy of Tonatiuh
and its gift of consciousness.
The energy spits from her, becomes venomous.
The ordinary man cannot conserve it or utilize it.
But he who searches learns to turn the serpent inward
and the serpent wounds the enemy that it carries within itself.

---

* The 1995 text reverses pages 10 and 11 as they are presented on the 1961 recording. Because
the order of the pages on the recording seems more consistent with the flow of concepts and
because it represents the earliest arrangement we have, I opted to follow it in this version.

It shoots within and without and creates the two-headed serpent.
The hero learns a great secret by knowledge,
effort, sacrifice, and love.
He sheathes his serpent incisors
and makes her swallow her own venom.
And from the digestion of this venom grows the wings of the
spirit.
Quetzalcóatl, the Plumed Serpent, has been born in him.
He moves between gods and men.

31　Quetzalcóatl is also the planet Venus.
He is one of the trinity with Itzpapálotl (Obsidian Butterfly)
and **Tlahuizcalpantecuhtli** (Lord of the Morning).
As Itzpapálotl governs the new growth, the death,
and the rebirth of creatures, so Quetzalcóatl governs the growth,
the death, and the rebirth of the souls of men.

Fig. 4.5. Quetzalcóatl, "the link between gods and men"

[Page 11]

1   There is an occult energy in the heart that comes from Tonatiuh,
     the Sun, and if man releases it, returning it consciously to the
       Sun,
     he becomes immortal.
     But to liberate this energy, sacrifice is necessary.
     Man must sacrifice the desires and habits that he adores,
     sacrifice them in himself, and turn the knife against the enemy
     that he carries within himself, that keeps his heart a prisoner.

8   In recent times men still remembered these words,
     but they have now forgotten their significance.
     They have made enemies of other men

to sacrifice them and tear out their hearts,
believing such offerings would propitiate Tonatiuh.
Such is their degeneration, such is their superstition.

14   When fear unites with knowledge, terrible things are done.

15   It is the self within ourselves that we have to sacrifice.
It is our own heart that has to be torn out of the false being
and offered to the light.

18   May Xiuhtecuhtli, Lord of Fire, burn my false being.
May **Itzli,** Obsidian Knife, liberate my heart.

[Page 12]

1   Terrible is Itzlacoliuqui, Obsidian Knife, Goddess of Sacrifice,
marvelous and terrible,
because the sacrificial knife liberates the blood in everything,
blood of the stoned criminals,
blood of the beheaded deer,
blood from the very stone that kills,
blood from the knife itself,
blood from the lance of power,
blood from the incense burner,
blood from the vital force that flies toward the Moon,
blood from the soul,
blood from the solar system,
the blood of every star.

14   What is the blood that connects stones with soul, men with suns?

15   It is the universal unity, the one creative principle crystallizing
into myriad forms,
and when liberated by sacrifice
it returns to unity.

19   Because to sacrifice is to act consciously,
to sacrifice that which will be taken away
is to deny the destiny that takes it.

22   Defraud Death by sacrificing Life;
because from the hand of the Goddess of Sacrifice that holds
the obsidian blade
sprouts the germ of Life to come.

*Fig. 4.6. The New Fire Ceremony at the end of the age,
from Codex Borbonicus*

[Page 13]

1   To sow life in the fires of sacrifice:
      Are the flames rising on the Hill of the Star, toward Cauhlacan?*
      Or is it my own heart that is afire?

4   The cycle of years is past—the waiting ended.
      Come—reunite, pilgrims, for the sky is in flames!
      From Xochicalco to Teotíhuacan the red spreads

---

* Because this page was transcribed from the recording, I was unable to identify and confirm the spelling of this place-name. Phonetically it is Cauhlacan, and its context implies a celestial or mythological connection. The geographical names in lines 6–8, however, suggest that it may be the name of a real city. It may refer to the Culhuacan in the well-known manuscript *Anales de Chauhtitlan: Historia de reynos de Culhuacan y Mexico*. Mythologically and cosmologically it clearly refers to the highest celestial city or domain.

one step, another step, and another,
only twelve short steps from the cave of the womb
to the final conflagration.

10   Now Cihuacóatl, Ehécatl, Chalciuhtlicue, and Xiuhtecuhtli
incendiate the *four elements.*
The seven planetary gods throw my constituent parts into the fire:
Tlaltecuhtli, my *bones;*
Metztli, my *viscera;*
Paynal, my *members;*
Itzpapálotl, my sweet *flesh.*
Huitzilopochtli adds my *passion;*
Tezcatlipoca, my *sorrow;*
Mixcóatl, my fragile *mind.*

20   The flames rage in consummation—
Rise, oh flames!
What light, what heat!
What great holocaust!
The smoke ascends and spirals. . . .
Obscurity disappears
as the flames rise to the throne of Tonatiuh,
the purest light.

Commentary

Introduction

My intention in this chapter is to share, through line-by-line analysis, some pointers to a deeper understanding of the text of the Pyramid of Fire. Of course, my own exegetical elucidations might not correspond with the insights perceived by readers on their own. This, however, is to be expected with any multidimensional initiatory text from which insights of many different kinds may be gleaned by its readers. But whatever the differences in our discoveries, we can certainly agree upon some general points. For example, page 1 and page 13 involve *creation* and *apocalypse* (or more precisely, *ekpyrosis*, universal dissolution by fire), respectively. This frames the alpha and the omega of a grand cycle of manifestation and final re-absorption into the unmanifest godhead (Tloque Nahuaque).

To elucidate the codex, clear and discerning analysis is important, but to put analysis in its proper place, we should remember Marty's own emphasis on the power of poetry and the dramatic performance of the Pyramid of Fire. It is this evocation of gnosis that plants the seeds of wisdom into receptive souls for future flowering.

We should also recall that the text of the Pyramid of Fire is based on an authentic pre-Conquest-era picture book. In the same way that ancient performers of the dramaturgy used picture books as memory devices, so too did Marty's Mazatec friend. Daniel, who descended from a noble family that hid this codex and passed it down through the generations, is the modern-day dramaturgist. We might expect, however, that more than 450 years of retelling would result in some adaptations and alterations, though given that performance of sacred texts is essentially a conservative religious art and that each generation had the benefit of the pictures to provide the story's standard form, any changes that may have occurred were probably minimal. It should be noted that the Pyramid of Fire is unique in one important respect when compared to other Nahuatl picture books analyzed by scholars: It has been told by one in the lineage who is thereby privy to inner nuances and subtleties that can so easily escape an outsider's analysis.

The cosmology, however, that can be reconstructed from the Pyramid of Fire is generally consistent with that found in other Central Mexican codices[1] and appears in the text on many levels. First—and entirely serendipitously—after applying line breaks to the text, my transcription of the Pyramid of Fire resulted in 365 lines. This suggests a theme patterned on astronomical cycles, a meaning already inherent in the codex, given that it has 13 pages (13 is a numerological symbol for the moon's waxing from new to full), and is also consistent with a visionary recital and cyclical dramaturgy. We can also observe that the number 13 corresponds to the number of phases of the moon, and that the number of lines—365—also refers to the days in a solar year. Add to these observations the fact that, from creation to conflagration, the codex leads us through all stages in cosmogonic time. Thus it weaves solar and lunar rhythms, an interlacing that is the function of the 52-haab Calendar Round cycle that defines the timing of the New Fire ceremony as well as the end-of-age conflagration. The codex calls it the weaving of the One and the Many. Such patterning is in good company, for the Mexican poet Octavio Paz intentionally gave his poem "Sun Stone" 584 lines to evoke the period of Venus.

It has been valuable for me, as the modern redactor of the Pyramid of Fire, to base my commentary largely on my initiatory relationship with the text, rather than citing supportive academic source material. In following this method I do not claim to be a Nahuatl tlamatinime; I am more of a visiting perennialist, seeking Sophia in her multifarious forms.

Marty especially wanted to emphasize the ways in which the Pyramid of Fire paralleled concepts in other traditions in order to illustrate how it is that the codex belongs to the perennial philosophy.

In many ways Marty was a westerner who went native both internally and externally. In his unique process of studying, living within, and being transformed by native traditions in different parts of the world, he developed a deep grasp of the metaphysical principles and spiritual truths shared by all perennial philosophies, including those found in the Pyramid of Fire. This deep understanding along with his skill at speaking Mazatec (and his fluency in Spanish enabled him to accurately transcribe and translate the readings offered by Daniel.

Marty himself had many specific insights into how the Pyramid of Fire was related to other esoteric traditions. He saw parallels to Chinese Taoism, tarot, and to ideas explored in G. I. Gurdjieff's philosophy called the New Way.

Taoist philosophy is based upon the dualism of yin and yang in relation to a third "pole"—the neutral background. Marty mentioned that Ometeotl is the "One God" of the Aztecs, and a king of Texcoco (Nezahuacoyotl) was the first Aztec who had the idea of a single godhead from whom comes physical manifestation. In the codex such a cosmogenesis proceeds not from 1 (unity) to 2 (duality), but directly from 1 to 3. There is a comparable Chinese saying: "From 1 to 3; from that the 10,000 things." This philosophical notion is equivalent to the Taoist conception that duality must interact against a neutral background—there cannot be only two; a neutral third must immediately exist, implying a trinity of creative forces.

Marty recommended some passages in *Fortune-Telling by Mah Jongg* by Derek Walters (a rare book he sent me) for connections between Chinese oracles and the Pole Star or Big Dipper. (Also see Eva Hunt's *Transformations of the Hummingbird.*) "Spinning the spoon" in Chinese divination is analogous to the imagery of the four Tezcatlipocas spinning with one foot on the Pole Star. The first part of Walters's book describes the astronomy and astrology of ancient China, which Marty found very similar to the system in the Pyramid of Fire. Comparisons can be made to other Eastern systems, including Sufi mysticism, Zoroastrianism (Gnosticism's and Manichaeism's *ekpyrosis* doctrine), and Hindu and Buddhist philosophy.

Another connection between Eastern philosophy and the Pyramid of Fire is the idea of worldly impermanence, which Marty mentions in his introduction to this book and which we will discuss further in chapter 6.

Marty also pointed out a relationship between the Pyramid of Fire and tarot, emphasizing that Aztec calendar cosmology could be mapped onto tarot cards. The general connections are obvious: In Aztec cosmology there are 13 heavens and 9 hell realms, a total of 22, which is the number of tarot images in some versions of the deck. There are 52 years in a Calendar Round, which corresponds to the total number of cards used in some tarot decks and in modern playing-card decks today. Although Marty suggested that several tarot archetypes (The Fool, High Priestess, Emperor, and so forth) compare to Aztec day signs, it is difficult to project the entire sequence of analogies because of the problem of the correspondence between Aztec deities and the regular day-sign symbols. One set of deity and day sign correspondences is evident in Codex Borbonicus and Codex Telleriano-Remensis and is discussed by Bruce Scofield in his book *Signs of Time*.[2]

Marty also perceived a relationship between the Pyramid of Fire and the ideas of G. I. Gurdjieff, an enigmatic philosopher from the Caucasus who traveled widely throughout the Near East and Asia in the early 1900s and became a teacher of consciousness-expanding techniques that are largely based on ancient spiritual beliefs. His work became available to the English-speaking West through books written by one of his students, P. D. Ouspensky. *Tertium Organum, A New Model of the Universe*, and *In Search of the Miraculous* explore progressive ideas in a field of spirituality that can best be called Gurdjieffian, or New Way.

Marty pointed out that *A New Model of the Universe* (English translation, 1949) contains a cosmogonic system, called by Gurdjieff the Ray of Creation, that is strikingly similar to the multileveled and tripartite cosmology described on pages 1–3 of the Pyramid of Fire. The parallel is less surprising than we might initially assume, because, as Gurdjieff himself stated, such teachings are "at the root of all ancient systems."[3] Gurdjieff introduces the Ray of Creation by first explaining why three forces are required for all phenomenon in the world to exist. The Law of

Three explains how the Unity of the Absolute transforms into Plurality: From the One emerge the Three. This insight is echoed in the ancient Chinese teaching mentioned earlier: "From 1 to 3; from that the 10,000 things." Gurdjieff also finds in Brahma, Vishnu, and Shiva the idea of three forces unified in the Absolute.[4]

The Ray of Creation is a multidimensional conception of the universe, a holographic model in which smaller scales of existence are nestled inside larger dimensions, all of which follow a law of correspondence that is compared to the eight-toned musical octave. The seven levels or dimensions, according to Gurdjieff, are: the Absolute, All Worlds, All Suns (the Milky Way), the Sun, All Planets, the Earth, and the Moon.[5] This, of course, is strikingly similar to the cosmogonic model found on the first page of the codex. The Pyramid of Fire goes further to elaborate microsystems on the earth, including nature music and human music, which each consist of eight levels.

In the codex (6:17–19), we read that the Moon eats the departed vital energy of un-actualized men; in a similar way the idea that the Moon feeds on earth's organic life is discussed in Ouspensky's book.[6] Apart from these and other specific comparisons, the general idea that the codex shares with Gurdjieff's Ray of Creation is that of "as above, so below," the so-called Hermetic adage that many ancient traditions took to be self-evident. Such a principle operates in conjunction with nested scales of manifestation in worldly processes. On page 1 of the codex the repeated phrase "within him is born" suggests that each level emerges from the previous one, like a set of nested dolls or fractal manifestations, as shown below.

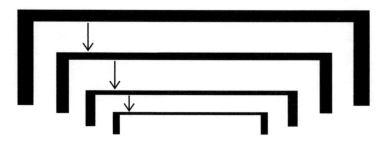

Fig. 5.1. Hierarchical orders of manifestation

This is exactly the same as the Law of Octaves that operates in the Ray of Creation teaching. Gurdjieff drew many of his teachings from his encounters with various Sufi masters throughout the Middle East, and Marty asserted that Sufi mysticism is "remarkably similar" to the teaching in the codex.

Commentary

Pages 1–5 of the Pyramid of Fire enumerate the many worlds and their processes, including the calendar cycles of the planets and the three cosmic principles, best described as male, female, and a neutral mediator.

Page 1:
Creation and the Celestial Hierarchy

1:1–29. The entire first page describes a celestial hierarchy that can be distilled into the following chart.

TABLE 1: THE EIGHT SUBDIVISIONS OF THE HIGHEST COSMOGONIC REALM	
1. Tloque Nahuaque	Lord of Intimate Vicinity
2. Tonacatecuhtli	Lord of Our Sustainment
3. Tzitzímime	Giants from Milky Way
4. Tonatiuh	The Sun
5. Sons and Daughters of Tonatiuh	the planets
6. Xochiquetzal	Nature
7. Metztli	the Moon; Earth + nature
8. Mictlantecuhtli (from 3:30-33)	Hell Worlds or Underworld

These are the eight subdivisions of the cosmos. In principle, each level can be further subdivided into micro-scale systems of eight subdivisions, although page 2 details only the subdivisions of the lowest three levels.

Page 2:
Harmony of the Spheres; "As above, so below"; and the Limited Vision of Man

Each level of the cosmos can be thought of as a domain or, following Neo-platonic terminology, a sphere. In this page we see that the structure of the individual spheres reflects the eight-level structure of the larger cosmos. Thus, a "Harmony of the Spheres" concept is implicit, referred to in the codex as a "cosmic musical scale" (2:4).

2:1–13. The eight subdivisions of each of the three lower levels of the cosmogonic realm are compared to the eight tones of the musical scale, suggesting a harmonic (or octave) relationship between the lowest and highest levels. We may call the eight cosmic divisions on page 1 the *Cosmic Music*. On page 2 we find further details about three other "music" levels:

TABLE 2: THE EIGHT SUBDIVISIONS OF THE THREE LOWER COSMOGONIC REALMS		
SOLAR MUSIC	NATURE MUSIC	HUMAN MUSIC
1. Sun	1. Heroes	1. Spirit
2. Saturn	2. Men	2. Heart
3. Mars	3. Animals	3. Head
4. Mercury	4. Insects	4. Semen
5. Moon	5. Plants	5. Blood
6. Earth*	6. Ground	6. Viscera
7. Jupiter	7. Rock	7. Nerves
8. Venus	8. Metals	8. Bone

*List is incomplete; it presumably includes Earth, Jupiter, and Venus (from 1:20–21, 23).

Thus, there are four cosmogonic levels that mirror each other, following the principle of "As above, so below":

       I. Cosmic Music
      II. Solar Music
      III. Nature Music
      IV. Human Music

2:14–17. Because it follows this principle, the universe "is Tezcatlipoca, Smoking Mirror" (2:16), a place where humans don't see clearly. Human beings are incarnated, living, and thus subject to the laws of birth and death. The world is a finite manifestation, a limited reflection of the infinite godhead, Tloque Nahauque, and therefore normal human vision and understanding is diminished like smoke on a mirror. In the Popol Vuh, the Quiché Maya creation myth, the same situation is described as "breath on a mirror."[7]

Page 3:
The Trinity Principle and the Domains of the Universe

Page 3 explicates the three phases of the deities of each of the subdivisions of the Cosmic Music (except for the subdivisions 1 and 4, which have only one deity each).

3:1–33. The first line on this page defines a perennial principle: all things of heaven and earth are created by three forces. The following lines expand on the operation of this principle, illustrating how the deity that rules each subdivision of the Cosmic Music consists of three phases or aspects (excepting subdivisions 1 and 4, which are stated to have only one deity each). The three "forces" or aspects are defined in two ways:

    . . . one masculine, one feminine, and one mediator;
    one active, one passive, one impartial. (3:6–7)

The three lowest "music" levels can also fit into this scheme: Solar (masculine), Nature (feminine), and Human (mediator).

There are eight levels of Cosmic Music. Each level is ruled by a deity. Almost every deity consists of three forces (phases or aspects). The deities on levels 1 and 4, however, are stated in the codex to be "only One"(3:8 and 3:17). The following table arranges the three aspects of each deity according to the names and genders given for them on page 3 of the codex. It should be noted that the stated genders of Metztli and Tecciztécatl are not consistent with the genders of those deities recognized in academic sources. They are placed here according to the gender scheme laid out in the codex. Although there are clearly eight levels, each deity is numbered to show that there are a total of twenty deities (because the deities on levels 1 and 4 are not tripartite). The importance of deciphering the presence of exactly twenty deities in the cosmogonic structure of the Pyramid of Fire lies in the fact that these twenty deities rule the twenty day signs of the Aztec calendar. They are not the day-sign names themselves but secondary rulerships.

TABLE 3A: THE THREE PHASES OF THE DEITIES OF THE COSMIC MUSIC

MASCULINE	MEDIATOR	FEMININE
1.———ONLY TLOQUE NAHUAQUE (1) IS ONE———		
2. Tonacatecuhtli (15)	Ometecuhtli (2)	Tonacacíhuatl (9)
3. Centzonhuitznáuac (16)	Tzitzímime (3)	Centzon Mimixcoa (10)
4.———ONLY TONATIUH (8) IS ONE———		
5. Tlaltecuhtli (17)	Coatlicue (4)	Tlazalteotl (11)
6. Xochipilli (18)	Centéotl (5)	Xochiquetzal (12)
7. Metztli (19)	Tecciztécatl (6)	Coyalxauqui (13)
8. Mictlantecuhtli (20)	Teoyaomiqui (7)	Mictecacíhuatl (14)

When we codify the arrangement of table 3A into a number sequence using the numbering to the right if the deity names, the following arrangement results:

**TABLE 3B: THE THREE PHASES OF THE COSMIC MUSIC DEITIES
CODIFIED INTO A NUMBER SEQUENCE**

	1	
15	2	9
16	3	10
	8	
17	4	11
18	5	12
19	6	13
20	7	14

The middle column corresponds to the mediating or neutral deities. The column on the left corresponds to the masculine or active deities. The column on the right corresponds to the feminine or passive deities. Deities 1 and 8 are special because they "are One" and have no partners in the scheme of triplicities. This table is a simple representation of the cosmogony described on page 3 of the codex and can be represented visually with the following diagram.

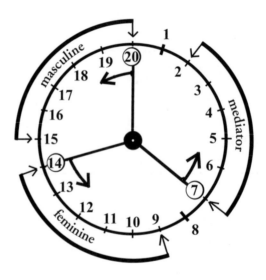

Fig. 5.2. Triplicities and the twenty day signs

The triplicities can be correlated by moving counterclockwise around the chart. The example shown indicates the trinary deities of 7, 14, and 20: Teoyaomiqui (7), Mictecacíhuatl (14), and Mictlantecuhtli (20). These three deities are the masculine, mediating, and feminine aspects of the eighth subdivision, as can be seen by referring back to table 3A. Of the eight subdivisions, only six partake of the tripartite scheme. If we thereby disregard levels 1 and 4 (because they are "only One") levels 2 and 3 appear paired. Consequently, by structural analogy we can likewise pair levels 5 and 6, as well as levels 7 and 8, and derive three paired levels as in the following table:

TABLE 3C: PAIRING OF LEVELS IN THE EIGHT SUBDIVISIONS

XXXXXXXXXXX		
1	1	1
1	1	1
XXXXXXXXXXX		
2	2	2
2	2	2
3	3	3
3	3	3

The point of this structural analysis is to show how the topic explored on page 4 of the codex, the six classes of divine game, is a logical outgrowth of the text on page 3. It is helpful to visualize the encoded information with the aid of these diagrams, for they reveal a structural evolution characteristic of the unfolding cosmos itself. We are thus led to see not only a tripartite division of six of the eight subdivisions, but also the pairing of the six tripartite subdivisions into three groups. (Note: The phrase "six classes of divine game" is used here in the same sense that we use "five aspects of Hindu religion": divine game [singular] is subdivided into six classes.)

Page 4:
Six Classes, Four States of Matter,
and Four Seasons of Time

> Each world is the play of three gods,
> three forces and their field of action. (4:1–2)

4:1–9. Combining the three forces in all their permutations gives rise to six classes of divine game. The order of the three forces—masculine (A in Table 4), mediator (B), feminine (C)—defines the six classes that the codex lists as growth, decadence, purification, infirmity, curation, and regeneration (4:7–9). The classes can be paired to reveal three primary types of activity, as shown in the following table.

TABLE 4: THE SIX CLASSES OF DIVINE GAME

FORCE (MASCULINE MEDIATOR, FEMININE)	DIVINE GAME	TYPE OF ACTIVITY
A B C	Growth	Growth and regeneration
C B A	Regeneration	
B A C	Decadence	Decadence and infirmity
C A B	Infirmity	
A C B	Curing	Curing and purification
B C A	Purification	

Notice that the order of the three forces in each pair are mirror images of each other. For example, A-B-C (Growth) is paired with C-B-A (Regeneration). The importance of this patterning is that it reveals a self-consistent and logical, yet deeply hidden, structure of the codex. The lines on page 4 that imply this interpretation seem poetically inspired and we wouldn't suspect them to contain such a coherent cosmological structure, and yet a careful parsing out of each line reveals important insights. The six classes, grouped into three paired phrases, can further be distilled into three terms:

Increase (growth and regeneration)
Decrease (decadence and infirmity)
Healing (curing and purification)

We can presume that whichever of the three forces is playing the role of mediator (the letter in the middle of the three in the first column of table 4) is the key to identifying which divine game is being played. Thus, when B, the mediator, is in the middle, everything is in balance and growth and regeneration *(increase)* result. When C, the feminine, serves as mediator, a situation of purification and curing *(healing)* results (primarily because women were healers and herbalists in Aztec culture). When A, the masculine principle, mediates, decadence and infirmity *(decrease)* result. (History has shown that a dominating patriarchal culture leads to territorialism, warfare, and degeneration.)

The six processes create "all which occurs or may occur." These permutations are finer divisions of a trinary cosmology that we might compare to the three principles of Egyptian sacred science, which are based on the square roots of 2, 3, and 5.[8]

4:10–19. The three forces are governed by four states of matter, four deities, and four seasons or time divisions. Table 5 clearly illustrates the deity/matter governance relationships.

TABLE 5: DEITIES AND STATES OF MATTER

DEITY	FORCE/TYPE OF MATTER
1. Xiuhtecuhtli, Lord of the Year	Active, masculine matter: Fire
2. Chalchiuhtlicue, She of the Jeweled Crown	Passive, feminine matter: Water
3. Ehécatl, God of Wind	Impartial, unifying matter: Wind/Air
4. Cihuacóatl, Woman Serpent	Inert, current matter: Earth

Notice in the table that the elemental states of fire, water, and wind/air are *dynamic* matter states, whereas earth is called an *inert* current (or conduit) of all forces (4:18–19).

4:20–29. These lines introduce the four states of time (the four seasons) and the four deities who govern them.

TABLE 6: DEITIES AND THE SEASONS/STATES OF TIME THEY GOVERN

DEITY	MATTER/FORCE	SEASON/STATE OF TIME
Xiuhtecuhtli	Fire/masculine	Spring/Xipe Totec
Chalchiuhtlicue	Water/feminine	Summer/Tláloc
Ehécatl	Air/mediator	Autumn/Chicomecoatl
Cihuacóatl	Earth/inert	Winter/Itzlacoliuhqui

Let us recall how valuable it was to combine, in table 4, the three forces (A, B, and C) in all their different combinations. We diagrammed the permutations (or total combinations) to reveal the construction of the six classes of divine game. Here, in tables 5 and 6, the three forces combine with the four seasons and the four elemental states of matter. Earth (corresponding to winter) is designated an *inert* state of matter, however, so earth's combination with the three forces yields three *passive* states. Consequently, we can diagram the permutation of the three forces with the remaining three dynamic seasons/states, to generate a total of nine *active* states. Thus, nine active states, plus three inert states, total twelve states.

TABLE 7: NINE ACTIVE STATES AND THREE PASSIVE STATES

	MASCULINE	MEDIATOR	FEMININE	DIRECTION	
Spring/Fire	1	2	3	East	
Summer/Water	4	5	6	South	9 active states
Autumn/Air	7	8	9	West	
Winter/Earth	10	11	12	North	3 passive states

This scheme can be simplified into a diagram resembling the Tree of Life in the Kabbalah, or system of Jewish mysticism, with the earth as the collective root:

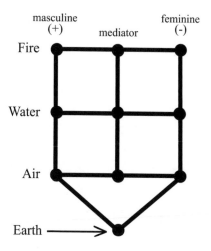

Fig. 5.3. The interaction of elements, seasons, and space

This representation depicts how the three forces (masculine, mediator, and feminine) combine with four temporal quarters and the four states of matter. Also, we may presume that spatial considerations are implicit in this model, since the four temporal seasons always correspond to the four cardinal directions in Mesoamerican cosmology. The text can thereby be understood as providing insight into the interrelatedness of space and time, a profound viewpoint that Western science attributes to the theories of Albert Einstein.

Table 7 and figure 5.2 generate important visual illustrations of how space and time are interwoven on page 4 of the codex. In addition, the integration of this "unified space-time" model with the four elements and the three forces suggests a profound understanding of natural processes, including those affecting Earth cycles and the inner life of humanity. This connection between natural processes in the environment and the inner, spiritual, unfolding of humanity can be explained only by the presence of universal principles, and is the basis of oracular systems such as the Chinese I Ching.

Page 5: The Calendar and World Ages: Consciousness of the Rhythms of the Gods

Tonalpohualli is the Aztec name for the 260-day sacred calendar, which the Maya call the *tzolkin* (count of days). According to the text of the codex, the 260-day cycle is based upon the cycles of Mercury, Venus, and Mars, which are as follows:

Mercury: 117 days
Venus: 585 days
Mars: 780 days

Parallel to this runs the solar year (365 days). The planets are the Divine Many and the solar cycle is the Divine One. Just how the 260-day cycle is the key to the other planetary cycles becomes clear when we look at their numerical relationships:

$$260 = 2.25 \times 117$$
$$260 = {}^4/_9 \times 585$$
$$260 = {}^1/_3 \times 780$$
$$260 = {}^2/_3 \times 390 \text{ (Mixcóatl)}$$

The 390-day period in the last equation above probably refers to Saturn. The synodic cycle of Saturn is actually 378 days while Jupiter is 399 days; perhaps this 390-day cycle represents an average of the two? Or, more likely, the Saturn period was approximated in order to allow a simple mathematical relationship with 260. We know that the Maya approximated the four phases of the Venus cycle for the same reason.

The codex tells us that after 9 × 260 days, Mercury, Venus, and Mars unite (5:36–37).

After 73 × 260 days, the Holy Year of the Planets (5:40–41) coincides with the Sun (this is the Calendar Round period of just under 52 years).

After 108 × 260 days (roughly 77 years), the rhythm of the inner planets unite with the outer planets (Saturn and Jupiter). Such is the duration of a person's life (28,080 days). Here we see an important connection between the cycles of the planets, the 260-day sacred cycle, and the human life cycle.

After 657 × 260 days (657 is corrected from 767), the cycles of the minor planets and the cycle of the Sun end together. This is 468 years, the duration of a culture. (The text says 767 Tonalpohualli, but this doesn't work out for the mathematical context given. I've taken the liberty to change this to 657 tonalpohualli. As mentioned in the footnote on page 74, 657 is given in early-1960s recording of Marty's reading.)

It is easy to see how all the smaller cycles fit into the period of 468 years, which equals 170,820 days:

$$
\begin{aligned}
468 \text{ years} &= 170{,}820 \text{ days} \\
170{,}820 \text{ days} &= 117 \text{ (Mercury)} \times 1{,}460 \\
&= 260 \text{ (the tonalpohualli)} \times 657 \\
&= 585 \text{ (Venus)} \times 292 \\
&= 780 \text{ (Mars)} \times 219 \\
&= 365 \text{ (Sun)} \times 468
\end{aligned}
$$

This period of 468 years is 9 Calendar Rounds, the period of an age of civilization. Such an accounting is found in other Central Mexican picture books. Tony Shearer, the author who is responsible for dating the famous Harmonic Convergence event of August 1987, identified 1987 as the year when the nine hell realms would end, because 1987 is 468 years after the year that Cortés arrived (1519).[9] However, the tracking of a Calendar Round should begin with a known New Fire ceremony, because New Fire ceremonies always occurred at the end of a Calendar Round. We have it on record that the last New Fire was performed in 1507; thus 1975 would have been the end of the nine hell realms.

The calendar portion of page 5 shows that celestial cycles and human cycles are related, and the key that unites the celestial and human realms is the 260-day tonalpohualli. In understanding these rhythms, we understand the rhythms of the gods—the divine principles that guide human spiritual unfolding.

Now we can engage in some philosophical reflections on the contents of page 5.

5:1–6. We are compelled to war, love, and do what we do by the "rhythm of the great gods." This is presented as a truth: First, seekers must understand that they accomplish nothing by themselves, that they owe all they are and do to a greater being and are intimately related to everything through higher cycles and larger forces. With this admission, they can learn to serve "the gods," (i.e., the planetary energies that inform the Earth). Human beings can become conscious of the rhythms of the planets.

5:7–23. The sacred calendar of 260 days is the key to the astrological mirroring of the celestial and human realms. The 365-day solar cycle is the mundane agricultural calendar that structures the exoteric dimension of human experience. Together, however, these two cycles form the One and the Many and combine to generate a union of the sacred and the secular, the esoteric and the exoteric, in the 52-year Calendar Round.

5:24–30. The 365-day Year of the Sun operates "parallel" to the 260-day tonalpohualli; together they represent a double play of divinity, one secular and one sacred, one the play of the Many, one the play of the One. The fact that these two realities, the Many and the One, are seen to operate in tandem is a profound conception in Nahuatl metaphysics. It reconciles a logical contradiction that troubles many philosophies. The Many are fragments of the One, but even in a fragmented state they retain a solidarity of intent and action with the primal state of Unity. A closely related conception may be found in the Tzutujil paradigm of *Jaloj Kexoj* (hah-low kay-show). In my book *Mayan Sacred Science* (Boulder, Colo.: Four Ahau Press, 1994) I explain this concept as a combination of two processes of change, one based on "flowering" or replications of a primal unity at successive scales of unfolding, and one characterized by "multiplicity" or the binary expansion/fragmentation of a system's elements as it evolves. The entire conception is based on the Tzutujil creation myth called "Flowering Mountain Earth."[10]

5:36–39. It is somewhat unusual in Mesoamerican calendars to point out that 9 tonalpohuallis (2,340 days) allow a commensuration of the cycles of Mercury, Venus, and Mars. The period is 6.41 years.

5:40–45. The New Fire is kindled at the end of every 52-year Calendar Round period. This is consistent with the New Fire tradition, and according to the chronicler Sahagún, it involved rekindling fire from the chest of a sacrificial victim when the Pleiades passed through the zenith precisely at midnight. At this moment the sun is at nadir, thus the solar fire is pulled up from under the earth while the Pleiadian light is brought down, creating a kind of axis of energy running from nadir to zenith. The codex refers to the New Fire as the "son of the Sun," which makes sense because it initiates a new Calendar Round cycle and all the fires in the city and outlying regions are relit from it.

5:46–50. It is stated that 108 tonalpohualli is the duration of a man's life. The number 108 is sacred to Buddhists and Hindus as well. The period of 108 tonalpohualli is almost 77 years.

5:51–55. Here we learn the duration of an age, the life of a culture. It is equal to 468 years or 9 Calendar Rounds, when all the planets and cycles shine together in the same form, that is, meet again at their beginnings. This period is found in other Central Mexican World Age accountings. The idea that planetary cycles combine to make a large cycle—a World Age—is the preferred perspective of the Central Mexicans, who favored the Calendar Round and its attendant New Fire Ceremony as the way to track and calculate World Ages. This method began with the Teotihuacanos around 312 C.E. and continued to be used by the ninth-century Toltecs of Tula and the fifteenth-century Aztecs. The last reported New Fire ceremony occurred in 1507.[11] By comparison, the Maya used the Long Count calendar and considered the precession of the equinoxes to be the determining factor in calculating World Ages.

The first five pages of the Pyramid of Fire have a certain completeness unto themselves. With page 6, the narrative shifts, and we find that pages 6–8 teach the esoteric, yogic secrets of spiritual awakening and ascent.

Page 6:
Sun and Moon, Two Classes of Men,
and the Meaning of Sacrifice

6:1–6. The Sun and the Moon rule over Earth. The various domains of nature include two classes of humans, which can be described simply as "conscious" and "unconscious," or "internally oriented" and "externally oriented." The externally oriented human is lost in the world of appearances and cannot see the essence within that connects all phenomena and defines all relations. The superior (internally oriented) human is on a path of deepening insight and utilizes penance and sacrifice to open the "wings of the soul." For cultures that value hedonism (modern American consumer culture, for example), this teaching sounds highly undesirable. Such a teaching, however, is found in many spiritual traditions: Spiritual growth requires a sacrifice. Psychologically speaking, personal sacrifice involves transcending or "putting into perspective" self-interest, so that a higher truth can be served. It is all about letting go, transcending the ego, and dissolving boundaries. It is not about feeling guilty or being "holier than thou" or seeking penitential pain, although disentangling ourselves from our addictions and immature desires can give rise to suffering. This is, however, a divine suffering that unfolds the "wings of the soul," a metaphor often found in Nahuatl religious poetry.

6:13–16. The man who makes offerings to the gods is in touch with the root and origin of all; he can act consciously and "truly is"—that is, he can become self-realized. In any person we can distinguish two selves called the lower self, and the higher self. The lower self is the ego identity consisting of all that relates to personality and identity. The higher self (sometimes referred to in the writings of Carl Jung as the Self) refers to the center and source of the individual being. The Self archetype, in Jung's terminology, is the center and totality of the psyche that continuously urges us to achieve wholeness. Mesoamerican Indians would call it the first ancestor, and through ceremonial offerings a two-way channel of communication could be opened with it, as well as with more immediate ancestors such as grandmothers and grandfathers.

6:17–26. The man who is attached to his lower nature, to his physical being that dies and is therefore time-bound and limited, will be devoured by the Earth in due time. This view is not unlike a profound text called *The Secret of Golden Flower* from Taoist secret teachings. In this human life we have a rare opportunity to develop a spiritual body through perfecting certain practices. The initiate is taught to conserve the vital fluid (sexual energy) and turn it inward to feed the creation of an immortal diamond body that will survive body death.[12]

6:27–31. The superior man develops his soul to become good food for Tonatiuh, the Sun. In other words, his soul is developed to be free and conscious so that it can be liberated by being fed to or dissolved into the unmanifest ground of being or unqualified light of Tonatiuh. The eating metaphor is a poetic way of referring to the dissolution of the incarnated being back into the unmanifest, eternal, and infinite ground of all manifestation—the "light" of Tonatiuh. Thus, like the maguey spines resting on their bed, the liberated soul can find its true resting place, the Hill of Heaven. This image suggests a high point of the sky, a cosmic center, the top of a mountain or pyramid. In addition, because Mesoamerican cultures saw the night sky as the underworld, the Hill of Heaven might also be seen as the deepest point of the underworld, which is the "death-door"—the portal into and out of the Earth realm. In this sense it can be equated with the "cave of creation" or the mother's birth canal.

Page 7:
Death, Spirit, and the Serpent of Consciousness

Pages 7 and 8 have excellent pictographs associated with them. In this case they are taken from the Codex Borbonicus. Studying the pictures while reading the text can help to clarify just how the picture books were used as memory devices for performing the contents of the codex.

7:1–6. Mother Earth is the recycler of all that dies.

7:7–13. The "entrance to the Kingdom of Matter" is a like the opening to a womblike cave; it is a portal or door. Tezcatlipoca is often associated with the Pole Star or the polar axis, but here we see him connected with other celestial features that point to a different part of the sky. Mesoamerican astronomy recognized three cosmic centers: the Pole Star, the zenith (the center of the sky, directly overhead), and the Galactic Center.[13] What can be said briefly is that the dark rift in the Milky Way, which is near the Galactic Center, was considered to be a portal to the Otherworld—that is, a birthplace in the sky. It also happens to be located at the crossroads formed by the Milky Way and the ecliptic; for Mesoamerican cosmologists such celestial crosses symbolized the concept of *center*. Without even emphasizing the Galactic Center, we can look at how the text describes Tezcatlipoca as a Falcon Herald of the Gods, wearing solar and Milky Way symbols. The only places where the sun and the Milky Way can join are at the two crossing points of Milky Way and the ecliptic, one in Sagittarius and one in Gemini. The one in Sagittarius— where the dark rift is located (the "entrance to the Kingdom of Matter")— is surmounted by the Hawk constellation called Aquila (the Eagle) in European astronomy. It is recognized as the Xic (Hawk) constellation by the Maya. The Falcon Herald, Tezcatlipoca, offers the (latent) wings of the soul to the newborn as a gift from the gods. In other words, the place in the sky pointed to by these features is the place of escape and spiritual freedom, the celestial Sun Door at World's End.[14]

7:14–17. These lines suggest that the human spinal column is a microcosmic reflection of the World Tree, a centipede that can sprout the wings of liberation. Another related metaphor, found in other Nahuatl poems, is the butterfly emerging from the cocoon. We see this portrayed on the beautiful Aztec statue of Xochipilli, the prince of flowers, and is symbolized by the statue's spiritual meaning.

7:18–23. The skull (bones), heart (viscera), and head (personality) are left to decay on earth after the soul (life force) has flown, returning to its source. This depiction can be stated simply as: though bodies die, life does not.

Fig. 5.4. Xochipilli, the Prince of Flowers

Page 8:
The Milky Way as the Spiritual Summit of the Tree of Life

8:1–2. Man treads a narrow razor's edge ("climbs the tree") between life (Tonatiuh, the Sun) and death, or Hell.

8:3–9. The four elements (at the base of the tree) and all the things in the basket, including the wings of the soul, are bequeathed at birth. These wings are latent in the newborn and must be developed before they can unfold.

8:10–14. These lines contain very important imagery. The door of disembodiment is the death door at the summit of the tree, where the transcendent Sun shines. This is the hypercosmic Sun into which all beings return. As lines from a poem called "Clouds" state: "We grow to crave each other's eyes, to be as one in mind / like clouds that die into the sky, love we all will find."[15] This death door is also the location of the

Fig. 5.5. The Midnight Sun, from the Borgia Codex

Midnight Sun that unites the four paths or roads that are almost always associated with the crossroads of the Milky Way and the ecliptic. The only "midnight sun" or "hypercosmic sun" that could be associated with this place and visible at midnight, is the Galactic Center.

Upon bodily dissolution, our various "mortal elements" and parts run to their own place, as listed in lines 16–20. These mortal elements each have their own specific gravity, we might say, and sift into discrete levels in the world hierarchy.

The solar energy within "the serpent" of consciousness is "the spirit" by which man is translated into the sky (the stellar world) at death. This imagery is consistent with the teachings of *The Secret of the Golden Flower*. The Milky Way (like the Hill of Heaven) is "above all"—that is, at the top of this cosmogonic hierarchy. And it is stated that the Milky Way consists of "innumerable suns." To say that the Milky Way consists of many little suns is an astonishing insight, but it was indeed possible for those who observed the heavens with the naked eye to understand this truth—the fourth-century B.C.E. Greek astronomer Heraclides of Pontus espoused such a theory.

Page 9:
Descending and Ascending Processes and the Wings of the Soul

This page presents several spiritual images within the metaphor of the hydrological cycle of water: Water evaporates and returns to the celestial realm of the clouds, then pours down again to begin the cycle anew. In all realms where ascent and descent occurs, Chalchiuhtlicue oversees the downward flow, while Tlaloc rules the upward ascent. Evaporation is an apt image for the dissolution and return of the soul into unity with the unmanifest ground of being, the transcendent light of Tonatiuh. In the text the down-up process is equated with man's forgetting and remembering, the divergence from (down) and return to (up) the celestial source. Pulque, an alcoholic beverage specified as the cause of man's forgetting, is used as a poetic device in the story of the fall and redemption of Quetzalcoatl. (See appendix 1 for a brief retelling of the myth.)

Time is the downward flow. The upward return to the source, on the wings of the soul, is a fight against time's current. The wings of the soul hide in the past because they were given at the beginning of life and must be reanimated; time's downward decay has eroded them. A regeneration or "backward flowing method" must be implemented, which is the method employed in the Taoist sacred book *The Secret of the Golden Flower*. This energy sublimation is taken up further on page 10.

Page 10:
Energy Sublimation and the
Awakening of the Divine Life

10:1–5. Quetzalcoatl is the redeemed or regenerated man, one who has experienced the apotheosis or visionary ascent/initiation into the divine light.

10:6–7. The inner circle is made up of those who are ascending the axis of spiritual unfolding, those who thereby link the mundane and transcendent realms through having opened or awakened the vertical conduit. This vertical conduit provides release from the horizontal flow of time and the vicissitudes of the cycle of reincarnation.

10:8–15. By activating the solar germ of consciousness *(coatl)* within his semen, man grows his spiritual wings. The lowly centipede transforms into a Plumed Serpent who can touch (or fly to) the spiritual heights.

10:16–30. Here we have uncompromising sublimation imagery. The energy that normally flows outward into material manifestation can be turned inward to fuel an involution of the spirit. It is consistent with Nahuatl spiritual philosophy to portray the outward flow of vital energy as spitting and cruel, because it is inimical to the re-absorption into light and the ultimate peace sought by those training to be Quetzalcoatls. Such a perspective is also found in Hindu, Buddhist, and Gnostic spirituality, and is often criticized as being world-denying. But the Bodhisattva vow of the enlightened being who chooses to remain in the world for the benefit of all beings implies that an enlightened being can exist in the world while transcending it in spirit. This is actually the natural state of a fully actualized being and is not world denying, but instead is simultaneously world embracing and world transcending. Contrary to popular (and even doctrinal) misconceptions, transcendence is inclusive of, not separated from, that which it transcends.

Through effort, sacrifice, and love, man turns his own "poison" inward and digests it and transforms it into spiritual vision. Celibacy is presented as an essential component of this path, a view that is shared in the true teachings of Tantra, but which is distorted by modern civilization, which is so enamored of its own sexuality. The secret truth is that sexual energy fuels a higher union and a divine pleasure. The codex expresses imagery that is equivalent to the Hindu story of the rape of a Nagi serpent-goddess (echoing the story of the theft of soma), in which Indra kisses the ugly snake, swallows the soma poison and transforms it into nectar, which results in the snake's transformation into a beautiful bride. In this sublimation story the transformation of the soul essence (soma) takes place in the heart and unifies Shiva and Shakti, the male and female currents in the body. The activated two-headed serpent can, at the same time, see inwardly and act outwardly in the light of that awakened inner vision. If not channeled in this way, sexual energy will instinctively spit outward and, lacking control, seek only the physical propagation of progeny. "He sheathes his serpent incisors" (i.e., refuses the outward release) and "makes her swallow her own venom" (sublimates the essence into his inner being). Thus the wings of the soul unfold. The somewhat violent energy is also found in the Hindu myth of the rape of the Nagi serpent and derives from the idea that the lower nature is consumed by (or subsumed into) the higher nature.

10:31–36. These lines are somewhat obscure. Quetzalcoatl is "also" the planet Venus and is part of a trinity of deities associated with Venus. The text tells us (10:34-36) that Itzpapálotl (Obsidian Butterfly; Venus as evening star) governs the growth, death, and rebirth of *creatures*, while Quetzalcoatl governs the growth, death, and rebirth of the souls of human beings. This indicates that Quetzalcoatl is a spiritual redeemer who, like Christ, knows how to resurrect/regenerate himself and thus can guide other souls to do the same. He oversees the second birth, the birth of the soul into a divine existence beyond dualities and the endless wheel of animal propagation.

Upon meditating on these lines I believe I've discerned what this distinction implies: Quetzalcoatl represents a higher aspect of Venus and may represent the Pleiades (or perhaps the Pleiades in conjunction with Venus). Although he later came to be identified with Venus, Quetzalcoatl's earliest association was with the Pleiades. He is first found at Teotihuacan in the third century C.E.[16] His role in the New Fire ceremony (such as at the

Pyramid of Kukulcan-Quetzalcoatl at Chichen Itza) and the central role of the Pleiades in the New Fire tradition support such a view. While his astronomical identification here is speculative, his archetypal role is clear: Quetzalcoatl oversees the spiritual rebirth of humankind.

Page 11:
Solar Fire Purification and Sacrifice

This page is essential to clarifying the Nahuatl understanding of sacrifice.

11:1–7. *Occult* here simply means "hidden"—a hidden solar/soul energy buried (imprisoned) by illusion and the impermanence of the body. The solar soul energy originates in the Sun—that is, in Tonatiuh, which is the visible conduit of the Unmanifest Being above the Sun, Tloque Nahuaque. Man can liberate his soul energy, but sacrifice is necessary. In becoming a Quetzalcoatl, the man "must sacrifice the desires and habits that he adores" (11:5) in order to finally return to his immaterial and absolute source, center, or origin. He must separate or differentiate the eternal heart/soul from the imprisoning matrix of impermanence that encases it. The sacrifice is a consciously willed, personal, inner sacrifice of the false identity that masks or obscures the true self, "keeping it a prisoner" (11:7).

11:8–13. These lines seem almost like an aside, but provide a clue to dating the codex. "In recent times . . ." must refer to a period just preceding the barbaric sacrifices of the terminal pre-Conquest Aztecs (some time in the late 1400s). For don Daniel to include this, he must be reading a mnemonic device in the codex itself that was specifically intended to warn of the danger of taking literally the doctrine of heart sacrifice, which would lead to "superstition" and "degeneration." Such a message in pictographic form might appear to be to the uninitiated eye an affirmation of literal heart sacrifice, rather than a warning to avoid it. We may wonder if the codices already interpreted by scholars portray a similar warning, and how it can be distinguished from an affirmation of literal sacrifice.

I have always felt that the criticism of Aztec sacrifice rituals as intolerable examples of human barbarity is hypocritical. In the late 1400s the Inquisition in Europe was headed by the ambitious Dominican prior Fray

Tomas de Torquemada. The Inquisition, founded and authorized by the Pope's decree, used paid informers, armed enforcers, and a reign of terror to mount a campaign of annihilation against Jews and other "heretical groups" in Spain and Portugal. Thousands of people died, including women, the elderly, and children. Hundreds of thousands were dispersed to marginalized domains on the Continent.[17] And this was only one chapter in the Inquisition's 200-year love affair with torturing and murdering Europe's undesirables. The Catholic Church sponsored similar atrocities against Native Americans after Europeans arrived in the New World.

In Nahuatl religious poetry we often find a distinction between good magic and bad magic. Even during the phase of Aztec civilization when human hearts were being torn out without any spiritual intent, we can suspect that the true teachings were still known and practiced in some sectors. Any high culture—including our own—engages simultaneously in the full range of human activities, from the grossest debaucheries to the highest epiphanies. Modern scholars and the media, often following the well-known journalistic motto "if it bleeds, it leads," have focused overmuch on one aspect of the Aztec and Mayan cultures and thereby continue to promulgate stereotypes of these cultures. Such limited perspectives prevent an accurate understanding of the deep and profound teachings of the Aztec and Maya, teachings that are subtle enough to require more focus and attention than the average person today is willing to muster. This situation speaks more for the degradation of modern civilization than for the degeneration of Aztec civilization.

11:14. As the Pyramid of Fire suggests, the result of such degeneration and superstition is "terrible," especially when "fear unites with knowledge." Here we are provided with a warning that knowledge and power can be used to provoke fear to control the masses. When such a practice arises among a civilization's leaders, as it did, for example, in Nazi Germany, tyranny runs rampant while freedoms are curtailed. This degenerate state signals the end-game of a culture on the brink of self-destruction.

11:15–17. These lines reiterate the impassioned refrain: The true, eternal heart made of the energy of Tonatiuh must be "torn out" of the false being and offered (sacrificed/returned) "to the light." This is followed by an invocation that presages the dramaturgy of page 13: "Lord of Fire, burn my false self!" In other words, "purify me to be a channel of the divine light!"

11:18–19. Reading carefully these two lines—"Itztli, Obsidian Knife, liberate my heart"—we can note that they reveal a distinct difference between real sacrifice, for which only an obsidian knife would be used, and the description of sacrifice in the condemnations of lines 8–13. In chapter 6 we will explore in more depth this distinction between literal and metaphorical sacrifice. Here in the codex these meditations on sacrifice are precursors to the New Fire sacrifice at the end of time that is the focus of page 13.

Page 12:
Universal Uniting Energy, Sacrifice, and Transcending Death

12:1–13. Marvelous and terrible indeed! "The sacrificial knife" of lines 1–2 must have a larger meaning here, because following in lines 4–13 is a long litany of things from which it liberates "blood" or soul essence—including the deer, the criminals, the lance of power, the incense burner, the soul, the solar system, and even "every star." The sacrificial knife might be the scythe of death itself, but not a normal death, for in lines 20–25 we are told to "defraud death by sacrificing life." In other words, a conscious sacrificial death *is* the sacrificial knife and yields a different result from a normal death, which is the destiny of all things on earth and in the universe that have been born and embodied but have not experienced *the second birth of the spirit*.

12:14–18. These lines are profound, revealing that "the blood" referred to here is not normal blood, but something like *chi* or *shakti*: "the universal unity, the one creative principle crystallizing into myriad forms." In other words, like the tonalpohualli and the year cycle (the combined calendars of 260 and 365 days), this blood is the One and the Many. The Maya call it *chul'el*—blood as a kind of universal chi flowing through everything. And it returns to Unity (to the unmanifest ground of being) when liberated by sacrifice. Why? Because "to sacrifice is to act consciously" and "to sacrifice that which will be taken away is to deny the destiny that takes it" (12:19–21).

This religious principle is not different from offering food to the deity before it is eaten (prayer before the meal) or the consecration of the symbolic wafer in the Catholic communion.

12:23–25. "[F]rom the hand of the Goddess of Sacrifice . . . sprouts the germ of life to come": This recalls the story in the Popol Vuh in which the hero twins are magically conceived. A goddess called Blood Moon wanders by the tree in which the skull of One Hunahpu is hung; she holds out her hand, he spits in it, and the hero twins are born 260 days later. Dennis Tedlock, a translator of the Popol Vuh, shows how this event occurs in the dark rift in the Milky Way near the cosmic cross of the Milky Way and the ecliptic and how it involves the three brightest night-sky luminaries: Venus, Jupiter, and the Moon.[18] These three perhaps form yet another celestial trinity.

Page 13:
End Time Conflagration and the Visionary Ascent

As mentioned earlier, this page was lost until Marty's friend sent me a tape of Marty's reading from the early 1960s. A remaining mystery, however, is the identity of the place-name in line 2: Cauhlacan.

The subject of page 13 is the New Fire ceremony and the ultimate sacrifice that must be made upon ascending the pyramid of fire and meeting with Divinity (Quetzalcoatl, God of Renewal). The fire is the fire of purification that burns the dross of all mortal desire and illusion. By consciously entering into the fire of death and transfiguration, death is defrauded.

13:1-3. Here we see the conflation or parallel meaning of the personal visionary ascent (in which death is a reabsorption into the unmanifest ground of being) and the universal conflagration at "the end of time." In keeping with the fiery conflagration imagery, the personal ascent is also described as a *burning* of a person's constituent parts.

This page is basically a description of the New Fire ceremony. The

World Age doctrine of the Aztecs required that the New Fire ceremony be performed at the end of every 52-year Calendar Round, timed by the Pleiades passing through the zenith at midnight. At this moment the sun is at nadir. In Aztec eschatology the world would come to an end if the Pleiades did not reach the zenith precisely at midnight.*

13:4–9. Here, the cycle of time has ended, and the fire of dissolution is spreading. This is the universal conflagration or *ekpyrosis* that is heavily emphasized in Gnostic eschatology and Jewish apocalypse literature. "Twelve steps" (13:8) implies thirteen stations, from "the cave of the womb" to the "final conflagration" (13:8–9). In fact a system of caves was found under one of the main pyramids at Teotihuacan, which is probably the womb-cave referred to here.

13:10–19. Now the process of disrobing/dissolution/sacrifice begins—all the mortal parts of the incarnate being are thrown into the fire, and it is the seven planetary gods, like some Mesoamerican Annunaki, that "throw my constituent parts into the fire" (13:12). This process is exactly like that which occurs in the Gnostic ascent, a connection we will explore more closely in chapter 6.

Marty long ago mentioned to me that page 13 involved the New Fire, as suggest by the use of the Hill of the Star and the context of ultimate world-renewal at the end of time—the end of the "period of waiting." The metaphysical connection of the seven planetary gods making the sacrifice is to the seven chakras being opened up by the "fire" of Kundalini (which, in the Mesoamerican ideology, is ruled by Quetzalcoatl-Kukulcan).

13:20–27. The tenor of the dramaturgy increases: "[T]he flames ragè in consummation!" And finally, "obscurity disappears" (the obscurity of the

---

* The New Fire ceremony was performed more than two dozen times beginning around 312 C.E., and yet the world did not end. The Pleiades failed to reach the zenith at midnight on the projected day as a result of precession, but this was adjusted for many times. In *Maya Cosmogenesis 2012* I explain the true nature of the New Fire as a tradition for tracking precession. A precession-based connection between the Calendar Round and Long Count might be evident in the fact that 73 tun equal 72 haab.

Smoking Mirror in which "man does not see clearly"—see 2:16–17). The occluded vision is purified "as the flames rise to the throne of Tonatiuh" (i.e., as the soul returns to its source)—the place of "the purest light."

What a beautiful expression of the eschatological apotheosis of soul and world! It is quite a dramatic vision of the New Fire ceremony—not just any New Fire ceremony (of which there were many without the world actually ending) but *the final one.** It marks the end of time, the end of the world, the end of the soul's endless round of reincarnation—the beginning of a higher life.

As a dramaturgy, or dramatic performance, the reading of the Pyramid of Fire is intended to transport the initiate into the experience described. This may be too much to ask for in the modern-day context, but in our reading of the Pyramid of Fire we can at least open up to the Nahuatl understanding of cosmology, astrology, yoga, calendar cycles, spiritual ascent, sacrifice, worldly impermanence—and our ability to connect with the transcendent and absolute Source of All. Such a pursuit is a central concern of all traditions that represent the perennial philosophy. Simply stated: all true knowledge comes from an ecstatic connection to the transcendent.[19]

Conversations with Marty

In late 1995, I recorded my phone conversations with Marty. In our discussions he clarified certain passages in the Pyramid of Fire and commented on ancient Mesoamerican methods of teaching sacred knowledge. He also shared difficulties in his work of transcribing and translating the text and some details about his relationship with don Daniel.

When I asked Marty why both Tloque Nahuaque and Tonatiuh were "One," he said "because they are both centers of complete systems." He

---

* The details of what this means require a careful reconstruction of the astronomical dimensions of the New Fire ceremony, which can be found in my book *Maya Cosmogenesis 2012.* Suffice it to say that the New Fire timing was successfully adapted, at least at Chichén Itzá, to correlate with the Mayan end-date of 2012.

preferred Tloque Nahuaque to be identified as the "Lord of the *Intimate Vicinity*" rather than "Lord of the *Close* Vicinity," as most academic sources have it. *Intimate* implies an immanence, an all-pervading quality that Marty saw in Tloque Nahuaque, whereas for him *close* retained too much of a spatial bias. His insight here is that transcendence is inclusive—that is, the *transcendent being* is not above or apart from the world. Although infinite and immaterial, it pervades all finite manifestation, thus the term *intimate* is more appropriate.

Divination was a topic that interested Marty a great deal. His travels in Mesoamerica and Asia allowed him to see parallels between oracles used in both places. In one of the Aztec myths Tezcatlipoca is the one-footed deity who dances around the Pole Star. Marty pointed to a similar Chinese interest in the Pole Star by reading a passage from a book entitled *Fortune-Telling by Mah Jongg*:

> At some stage in the development of the Shih it became a custom to spin a spoon round on its bowl, and observe the direction in which the handle pointed. No doubt generations of parents have before and since been irritated by their children discovering this little trick for themselves. The reasons for spinning the spoon on the Shih, however, were much more profound. The ancient Chinese astronomers used a quite different method of observation to that of the astronomers of Babylonian times. Of paramount importance in the Chinese celestial sphere was the Pole Star, and the constellation Ursa Major which pointed to it. To the Chinese this constellation, known in the West as the Great Bear, was known, and still is, as the Ladle. The configuration of the seven stars which make up the Ladle therefore had considerable significance; it was at least one of the most recognizable constellations in the night sky, and for this reason it was often found depicted on religious flags. It was natural, therefore, for this group of stars to be depicted at the centre of the Shih. The next step was the inclusion of an actual ladle as a spinning pointer—a tangible representation of a heavenly, and therefore mystical, phenomenon. . . . Then there came a dramatic innovation. The spinning spoon was replaced by a very

special kind of spoon, one that must at first have surely been regarded as having magical properties, for it was made from lodestone, and after it had been set spinning would always come to rest pointing in the same direction.[20]

The Chinese approach to gaining wisdom is similar to the Mesoamerican approach, with an emphasis on cultivating inner gnosis. Marty explained, "There was a mother source of esoteric mystical knowledge, and it spread across the planet. The big question is: What is the source of all this? There are different kinds of theories, but they miss the point. If you have experienced on your own any kind of direct knowledge through the universal source, then you know it's there."

Marty's criticism of education in Western cultures seemed right on target: "In Western schooling we take children and make them respond to authority, and this teaches you everything about the superficial aspects of things—weights and measures and the like— but none of that is really important. *Understanding* is what is really important—inner knowing— but that is not offered in Western education."

I asked Marty about teaching methods in ancient Mesoamerica, and his response related directly to the Pyramid of Fire. He said, "That question relates to Mystery Schools and initiation, which you had in Mesoamerica and in many other parts of the ancient world. Education in Mesoamerica involved going through a death in order to be born into knowledge. Symbolic death is the beginning of education, and this is a key to understanding the Pyramid of Fire codex."

Because the Mesoamerican approach to knowledge was so different from the basic assumptions of Western education, problems would clearly arise from Western scholars trying to interpret Aztec and Mayan documents. Marty was well aware of these issues, saying, "If you follow the academics you'll get confused because they all are offering different interpretations. For lack of native sources, you have to go to Spanish sources and to the histories of the Spanish monks. But the problem there is that they come from a cultural tradition that was so judgmental, and actually quite primitive intellectually. They had no ability to understand the philosophical importance of the native ideas."

Marty further observed that scholars can label something a "ceremonial object" and then everyone nods their heads and believes they know what it is. According to Marty, this was an example of scholars "using overconfident language," which leads to them "peddling erroneous ideas."

Given these problems, it seemed to me that what was so important about the Pyramid of Fire was that it was a direct reading of the pictographs. Marty said Daniel was "a quite different source for the knowledge of what the document is about. Daniel got his interpretation on a direct line from his grandfather—memorized on a straight descent from the Conquest period."

Marty was well acquainted with the academic literature and was quick to credit some scholars with being more tuned in than others. For example, he especially appreciated the work of Miguel León-Portilla, and said that the studies of Henry Nicholson were good for understanding some aspects of the Aztec deities.[21]

He also appreciated the views of a scholarly translator named John Greenway, who wrote an introductory essay to *A History of Ancient Mexico: The Religion and Ceremonies of the Aztec Indians*. Marty read a lengthy passage from Greenway's introduction that lamented a major problem in the transcription of Aztec literacy into English, taking as an example the Aztec word *amatlacuilolitquitcatlaxtlahuitl*.[22] Marty laughed, "How can you transcribe that into English?" His own work to transcribe the Pyramid of Fire must have met with similar difficulties.

The feeling in Greenway's commentary is that English is not as subtle or sophisticated as the Aztec language,[23] a claim that has also been made for ancient Sanskrit, which contains many more words, tenses, and inflections than modern English. The idea that Marty found so fascinating, and which resonated with his own convictions, is that modern languages are less complex and less capable of subtle conceptual distinctions than ancient languages. This of course also implies that the modern mind is less refined than the ancient mind—a heretical suggestion that challenges the myth of progress (the belief that modern man is in all ways more advanced and refined than ancient man).

According to Marty's belief, the Aztecs, Tibetans, the Eskimos, the Chinese—in essence, most of the ancient cultures—were "close to nature" and derived their wisdom by "learning about things directly," by having a gnostic approach to acquiring wisdom through direct inner experience. Such direct inner knowing can dawn through reading the Pyramid of Fire out loud repeatedly, pronouncing all the Aztec words clearly. The deeper meanings and interconnections of multivalent concepts will come alive, and realizations will occur. These are realizations about the universal, eternal principles that create, sustain, and devour life in all its myriad manifestations through time. Such inner realization confirms the universal teachings and insights of the codex.

6 Gnostic and Perennial Parallels to the Pyramid of Fire

Marty begins his introduction to this book with a quote from Aldous Huxley that defines the perennial philosophy as a universal wisdom that can be identified in many of the world's traditions. The quote comes from an introduction Huxley wrote to the Bhagavad Gita, in which he also listed the following four principles shared by all perennial philosophies:[1]

1. The entire world of phenomenal manifestation (including individualized consciousness) arises from an unmanifest, immaterial, Divine Ground.
2. Human beings are capable of a direct experience of the Divine Ground, and such an experience is a way of knowing superior to discursive reasoning.
3. Human beings possess a double nature made up of a finite ego self and an eternal divine self.
4. The purpose of human life is to reunite with the higher divine self, and that Supreme Identity is equivalent to the Divine Ground of all manifestation.

The Pyramid of Fire, representing Nahuatl cosmology and religion, fulfills all of these criteria. Thus, we must expand the Euro-Asian focus of Traditionalist studies to include Nahuatl metaphysics as a legitimate perennial paradigm.

Several key features of the Pyramid of Fire, explored below, illustrate how it contains hallmarks of the perennial wisdom, a term that refers to the universal and eternal wisdom. In the title of this chapter I have distinguished Gnostic from Perennial parallels because Gnostic literature requires some careful explanatory provisos before we can fully appreciate its parallels to the teachings in the Pyramid of Fire—provisos that address the criticism of Gnosticism as being nihilistic (world-denying) and dualistic (in which spirit and matter are thought to be irreconcilable opposites).

Two topics that we have explored include the oracular Aztec divinatory calendar and the Aztec eight-level cosmogonic scheme. Much has already been written about the Mesoamerican invention and use of divinatory calendars,[2] and divination with calendrical overtones is a universal tradition in and of itself (perhaps best formulated in the Taoist I Ching). In addition, we have examined the Mesoamerican eight-level cosmology in the context of Gurdjieff's Ray of Creation, and can draw parallels from it to other Neo-Platonic, Islamic, and Gnostic models of the celestial spheres, which usually have eight spheres, but sometimes have as many as ten or twelve. We could even discuss Dante's model in *The Divine Comedy* and Johannes Kepler's Harmony of the Spheres as examples of late applications of the same type of celestial cosmology. The word *cosmology* should be emphasized, for it differentiates a primordial appreciation for *cosmos-logos* (cosmic knowledge) from the later scientific obsession with *cosmography* (cosmos graphing), which seeks only to map the cosmos, not to understand it. In fact, the very title of Kepler's early seventeenth-century work *Mysterium Cosmographicum* set the stage for an unfortunate shift to a more limited scientific perception of the universe.

There are many parallels between the Pyramid of Fire and major and minor points identifiable in traditional cosmologies. As Marty himself said, the problem with examining the codex's parallels to other traditions is knowing where to stop. Those we will look at more closely here are:

1. The Hermetic principle of "As above, so below" (the foundation of astrology) and the holographic principle, "The microcosm reflects the macrocosm"

2. The notion that the Transcendent Deity is inclusive: the Lord of the *Intimate* (instead of *Close*) Vicinity highlights the idea that transcendence is inclusive of that which it transcends

3. The World Age doctrine and precession (e.g., the Vedic Yugas, and the New Fire/Calendar Round tracking method)

4. The three sacred science principles in Egyptian, Mayan, Taoist, and Finnish traditions

5. Impermanence (Taoism/The Book of Changes) vs. Gnostic nihilism; the non-dualistic (non-mutually exclusive) relationship between the finite and the infinite

6. Sublimation yoga (becoming a Quetzalcoatl)

7. The notion of sacrifice: self-naughting and self-sacrifice as drawn from Ananda Coomaraswamy's essays

8. Gnostic eschatology, including (a) Ekpyrosis (reference *Timaeus*, Berossus, and Seneca's *Naturales Quaestiones*) and (b) The visionary ascent (as a dissolution/disrobing), as in the context of Ezekial, *Poimandres*, and Innana

1. "As above, so below." This is a fundamental insight into the structural organization of the universe. Oddly, this principle is quite often dismissed as a primitive astrological superstition, but its meaning is simple: The processes and patterns in the sky parallel (or reflect) the patterns and processes on Earth. Life on Earth has evolved in a field of universal energy, is embedded within it, and the sky and Earth are intimately connected.

The principle "As above, so below" also involves pattern correlations between seemingly disparate dimensions of the natural world. For example, the branching patterns in lung tissue (the alveoli) are exactly the same as those found in leaves and those observed in the satellite imagery of river deltas. This example, however, may be better expressed as "The microcosm reflects the macrocosm." In other words, smaller scales reflect larger scales in the natural order. In modern mathematical theory this idea is in vogue in fractal geometries that can be graphically illustrated.

The reason why astronomical processes are believed to reflect processes experienced on Earth, including the subjective experiences of human beings, is because everything is united by the same root principle of unfolding. This is best illustrated by the "magic" number 260 in the function of the Mesoamerican sacred calendar of 260 days. Because it is the key factor uniting the sky and Earth, the number 260 represents "As above, so blow." This can be seen most clearly in the following observations:

The period of 260 days is associated by Mayan day keepers with human embryogenesis, that great cycle of human unfolding that we all share and that ends in birth. This process lies in the realm of human biology. The 260-day period is also the period between the planting and harvesting of corn in the Mayan highlands—an agricultural application. Most important, 260 days is the key used to predict such astronomical phenomenon as Venus risings and eclipses—an astronomical application. Thus, the processes in the realm of human unfolding on the Earth plane and in the celestial domain of the planets follow the same underlying patterning structure. (I have shown in my previous books that the Golden Ratio is the principle at the heart of the "magical" properties of the sacred number 260.)

"As above, so below" is called the Hermetic dictum because it is usually attributed to the Egyptian-Hellenistic prophet Hermes. Almost all ancient civilizations as well as traditional cultures surviving today assume that the processes of the sky and Earth are connected.

2. Transcendence is inclusive. In some theological circles, particularly in Christian discourse, the idea of a transcendent deity is quite often thought to mean a deity that is completely "other" or "above" or "outside" the created world. The stereotype comes to mind of a bearded Jehovah sitting on a cloud, occasionally deigning to glance down on His Creation to sling judgment. Or there is the more scientific notion of a creative impetus or force that jump-started the world (e.g., the Big Bang), which then has no influence while the world unfolds. This "clockwork universe" conception also speaks for a creative force, a *prime mover*, that exists outside the realm of the created world.

Nahuatl theology and metaphysics identified the highest creator deity as Tloque Nahuaque, who is the unmanifest Ground of all Being. This deity is the Lord of the Intimate Vicinity, meaning that it is always present, in all possible interstices of phenomenal existence, as well as being the ground or wellspring from which all manifestation arises. To transcend, then, is not simply to rise above or "go beyond" that which is transcended. Transcendence *is inclusive of what is transcended*; in other words, that which is transcended continues to be a part of the larger field within which all smaller orders of organization continue to be included. Such a clarification helps us to understand that higher dimensional beings do not exist in an altogether *other* order of existence; a five-dimensioned being contains within it the beings of the fourth and third dimensions. Some metaphysical teachings suggest that the three-dimensional world of Earth will cease to exist after human beings collectively ascend. Considering the principle of inclusive transcendence, these teachings are mistaken and are likely to generate fear.

The basic message of transcendence involves the relationship between the unmanifest ground of being and the manifest creation. This is the relationship between the infinite and the finite. It is very important to understand that these are not polarized, mutually exclusive opposites. On the contrary, the finite is embedded within the infinite as a latent possibility. In other words, finitude is one of the possible states that infinity can choose to be—if it were otherwise, it could not be considered infinite. The strict dualism of matter (outwardly finite) and spirit (essentially infinite) that is often ascribed to Gnosticism can thus be understood in the deeper sense that is taught in Nahuatl metaphysics. On a mythological level this teaching is encoded within the story of Quetzalcoatl's redemption (see appendix 1), in which consciousness loses itself (the infinite becomes finite) and then regains awareness of its essential ground, which is infinity or eternity. Infinity contains within it all finite manifestations.

Although we are elucidating here a teaching from the Pyramid of Fire, we again encounter an essentially Gnostic idea, that of the pleroma, the infinite plenum that holds within it all latent potentialities and underlies all manifestation.

3. The World Age doctrine. This concept, almost always found in perennial philosophies, is the idea that time moves in cycles and all processes in nature follow a cyclic pattern: birth, growth, decline, death, rebirth. It unavoidably has an astronomical basis and is closely related to the creation of calendars in ancient cultures. Given that the scale of

World Ages involves very large periods of time, we should expect to find a very grand astronomical cycle, and we do: the precession of the equinoxes. Precession, a slow stellar shifting caused by the wobble of Earth on its axis, is a period of almost 26,000 years. We find it to be at the core of World Age doctrines in Hindu, Mayan, Mithraic, Norse, and Egyptian traditions.

In previous studies I have argued that the New Fire tradition of Central Mexico, tracked with the Calendar Round, keeps track of a precessional shifting involving the Pleiades and the Sun.[3] As such, the eschatology we find on page 13 of the codex, because it depicts the New Fire ceremony, must ultimately be rooted in this large-scale celestial shifting. Generally, to find precessional knowledge in ancient Mesoamerican cultures is neither radical nor surprising, and has been discussed by various Mesoamerican scholars.[4] Without a doubt, eschatological theologies are linked to certain types of alignments that occur within the 26,000-year precessional cycle (see number 8, below).

4. The three sacred science principles in Egyptian, Mayan, Taoist, and Finnish traditions. In considering these we must first recall that in the Pyramid of Fire all things occur via three forces or principles.

Egyptian sacred science was explored by R. A. Schwaller de Lubicz *(Sacred Science)* and Robert Lawlor *(Sacred Geometry)*. While this subject is enormously complex, it is sufficient for this overview to state that Egyptian sacred science is based upon the three square-root principles (the square roots of 2, 3, and 5), which are believed in Egyptian cosmology to be responsible for the creation, maintenance, and dissolution of the world.

In his introduction to the Taoist *Secret of the Golden Flower*, Richard Wilhelm associates *Hsing* (human nature) with *Logos* and *Ming* (life) with *Eros*. These are the first two emergent principles and they correlate with yin and yang. We can assume that the Tao is the overarching primal Unity corresponding to *dios* (continuing the terminology we have used to identify the three principles).

These same three root principles operate within Mayan cosmology and calendars. In fact, a modern Tzutujil Maya paradigm of change called Jaloj Kexoj (hah-low kay-show), represents two of the three sacred root principles.[5] The key words for understanding this paradigm are *multiplicity* and *flowering* and, as I mentioned before, these two concepts can be equated with the codex's idea of the One and the Many united by the Calendar Round's two cycles: the 260-day sacred cycle and the 365-day year cycle. The third principle in Mayan time philosophy is the square-root 3 (1.733), which encodes the dynamic of the lunar eclipse rhythm (173.3 days) and all its philosophical overtones (such as the union of Sun and Moon, the union of opposites).

The trinity of principles found in Mayan sacred science is found in many different forms and can be identified by recognizing cognate symbols and translating parallel metaphors. Other traditions encompass these same principles. In Finland, for example, an ancient epic called the *Kalevala* tells of the adventures of three heroes. A Finnish mystic named Pekka Ervast interpreted the three *Kalevala* heroes as exemplars of three evolutionary principles in nature: Intellect, Emotion, and Will.[6] When we connect these anthropomorphized expressions of the three sacred science principles with the large body of Greek and Christian writings, they become Logos, Eros, and Dios—none other than the three principles of Mayan and Egyptian sacred science. It is startling to discover that such widely disparate traditions speak at their cores the same universal language of sacred science.

5. Impermanence. In the laments of Nahuatl poetry and song, it is recognized that everything on Earth is impermanent; everything must pass away. Nahuatl literature celebrates the beauty of flowers, the wondrous processes of nature, and yet does not ignore the insight that everything will eventually die or change into something else. This is the doctrine of impermanence that we also find in the Taoist Book of Changes, the I Ching. The world is a field of birth and death, of constant elemental transmutation, and the Nahuatl tlamatinime (poet-philosophers) were hungry for finding some eternal ground. The famous poet from Texcoco named Nezahualcoyotl (Hungry Coyote) lamented over having been born into the world of death and illusion[7] and wondered if a higher reality could be found. His hunger was satisfied with the nectar of cosmic vision born of poetry.

This Nahuatl worldview is not, however, nihilistic or world-denying, as we find in some Gnostic paradigms (such as in Manichaeism). Instead it is akin to the Taoist perspective: To embrace impermanence is to recognize the true state of *being in the world*, and is a necessary stage that leads to seeking beyond the veil of appearances for an eternal divine ground. The insight here is that, yes, the finite world of manifestation is *impermanent*, but the underlying divine ground that is the source of that finite manifestation is eternal and infinite—that is, *permanent.*

Tloque Nahuaque is the place of the Tao, the unmanifest ground underlying all phenomenal manifestation. And in the view of Nahuatl metaphysics, poetry and song give access to that divine source which, like the Lord of the Intimate Vicinity himself, is always present, interpenetrating, pervading, and shining within all phenomena if only the eyes can be opened to perceive it.

6. Sublimation yoga (becoming a Quetzalcoatl). Pages 10 and 11 of the codex describe this method by which the Mesoamerican initiate can become a fully actualized human being, a Quetzalcoatl, one whose spiritual wings are fully opened. Sublimation yoga requires "turning inwards the serpent energy" that resides within the semen. And by the inner digestion of this "venom" the wings of the spirit grow.

Without a doubt these pages describe the same method given in the Taoist *T'ai I Chin Hua Tsung Chih* (The Secret of the Golden Flower) and the *Hui Ming Ching* (The Book of Consciousness and Life). These sacred Taoist texts teach that an immortal spirit body can be generated by conserving the outward flow of seed energy (in the sperm) and sublimating it inward and upward through breathing and meditation. In this way a circulation of spirit energy creates a subtle "diamond body" that allows the spirit to fly to higher heavens at bodily death. According to tradition, this teaching originated in the eighth century C.E. when Lü Yeng (who folklore counts as one of the eight immortals) founded the Religion of the Golden Elixir of Life. The ancient oral teachings of this school were not recorded until many centuries later and became well known in Peking (Beijing). Lü Yeng attributes the esoteric teaching of *The Secret of the Golden Flower* to Kuan Yin-hsi, the same legendary master of Han-ku Pass for whom Lao-Tzu wrote down the Tao Te Ching.

Sublimation has taken on a slightly pejorative connotation through

Freudian sexual theories, in which nervous disorders are blamed on the backing up of unreleased sexual tension. Such a view is typical of early Western psychology, which had difficulty appreciating and integrating teachings like those in *The Secret of the Golden Flower*. Even Carl Jung, who wrote a commentary on Wilhelm's translation of *The Secret of the Golden Flower*, noted that many scholars mentally unravel upon encountering Eastern teachings, and warned that Westerners should not embrace *The Secret of the Golden Flower* as a viable practice. This is perhaps overly cautious and might apply more to the era when Eastern teachings first broke into Western consciousness. (Jung was writing in the 1920s.)

Then again, Jung's warning might be even more appropriate today because Western civilization is so obsessed with instant sexual gratification and sexual imagery is everywhere; it would be difficult to sustain the sublimation techniques taught in the sacred Taoist books. The West is more likely to pervert such teachings as a way to heighten or prolong sexual pleasure, as it has done with Tantric practices, which never intended the sacred couple to sexually consummate their *hieros gamos* (sacred marriage).

Sublimation as a way of unfolding the spirit is perhaps better known in the Hindu and Tibetan system of Kundalini yoga, which envisions the spine as a channel for the upward flow of evolutionary energy *(kundalini shakti)*. This main conduit is flanked by two other channels (or *nadis*) on the left and right, and the sublimated energy must circulate freely, as is suggested in *The Secret of the Golden Flower*. Interestingly, the Kundalini energy is called the "serpent power" and is presided over by a female deity, much like the teaching in the Pyramid of Fire:

> . . . he who searches learns to turn the serpent inward
> and the serpent wounds the enemy that it carries within itself.
> It shoots within and without and creates the two-headed serpent.
> The hero learns a great secret by knowledge,
> effort, sacrifice, and love.
> He sheathes his serpent incisors
> and makes her swallow her own venom. (10:21–27)

The key to these Eastern (and Mesoamerican) techniques of spirit-energy sublimation is celibacy. "Cessation of outflow" is the prerequisite for beginning the process of completing the Diamond Body. In Western culture celibacy is frowned upon as a highly questionable path and even when discussed, is almost never thought about as a spiritual pursuit. Among some it is valued in the sense of saving oneself for marriage, and it has achieved some status as a hip way to avoid STDs. In either case masturbation is generally allowed. Like the misuse of Tantric teachings, however, masturbation would defeat the spiritual purpose of celibacy in any sacred tradition. Nevertheless, refraining from sexual activity until later in life can contribute to full individuation by fueling the development of higher faculties that would otherwise remain dormant. When sexual relationships are thereafter pursued, individuals can bring themselves to these relationships as whole people, rather than as people who are codependent or emotionally stunted. It is probable that sexual activity at a young age, as so often occurs today, interferes with emotional and personality development, or at least delays or makes more difficult full individuation.

In Nahuatl sublimation yoga, the state of a fully actualized human being is imaged as a snake who has spread its latent wings. The Plumed Serpent, Quetzalcoatl, is a symbol uniting Heaven and Earth, bird and serpent, and can be considered equivalent to the union of Shiva and Shakti (avian and ophidian symbols) in Kundalini yoga.

7. Sacrifice or self-naughting. On page 11 of the codex, we find the line "Itztli, Obsidian Knife, liberate my heart" (11:19). As mentioned in the previous chapter, a literal reading of this line reveals a contradiction with the metaphorical meaning of sacrifice that we have identified (sacrifice your selfish attachments, give your "heart" to a higher purpose, and so on) because an obsidian knife could be used only for a real sacrifice. How can we understand this apparent contradiction?

The distinction is that one form of sacrifice, the form that is rightfully criticized, is inspired by a fear-based projection—rounding up unwilling enemies to kill and offering their hearts to the sun. The form of sacrifice that is noble and indispensable for personal ascent into the light and to feed the gods is a willing, conscious choice. And here is the hardest part for the modern mind not to reject instinctively: Both the noble and the fear-based forms of sacrifice can involve the actual sacrifice. In other words, in principle a successful sacrifice depends on the inner state, and the outer events are secondary. Whether the heart is literally or metaphorically offered is ultimately irrelevant; union with the divine is contingent only upon the inner state of the seeker. This goes completely against the grain of our moral teachings. But let's look more closely at this practice and our own culture's assumptions regarding it.

Our civilization condemns the consciously planned and expected sacrifice of lives—unless, of course, it is in service to a "higher cause" that our leaders deem worthy, such as a war. This "noble cause" is actually the same rationale that a willing Aztec initiate might employ. The intention behind our civilization's motivations, however, is often dubious, with private interest lurking behind the call to sacrifice. The Aztec cause, in its purest intention, is for the embracing of spiritual truth and a higher existence—that is, to feed the deity (the Sun, the source of life). As such, the intention is to feed the source of life rather than the deities of death, as when a call to war is made (no matter what kind of acceptable loss ratios are expected). In other words, our civilization accepts the sacrifice of life grudgingly with resistance, as a necessary evil in order to protect the agendas of capitalist materialism, whereas the Aztec sacrifice occurs with the conscious recognition of the interrelation of life and death. Which stance reveals the more conscious and advanced civilization? In the Aztec scenario, life and death are accepted as two poles of a higher unity. Modern Western civilization denies and resists death as an unwanted intruder and thereby ineluctably entangles itself more deeply in being in service to the deities of death (the shadow rather than the light gets the sacrificial offering). Such is the more extreme degeneration of any civilization on the decline, and it appears that the Aztecs themselves eventually debased their original teachings. Our culture could learn from this mistake.

The Mesoamerican ball game reveals a perplexing sacrifice tradition. In one version of the game, the winner was sacrificed. And the winner wanted to win. Shall we judge this as some kind of primitive delusion? Or can we accept it as being just as profound as eating the flesh of the deity, as in the Catholic communion? It makes more sense to offer to the gods a soul that has just accomplished something great, and is thereby proved to be the juiciest morsel for the god to consume.

One can imagine the cultural belief system that would have resulted in such a practice. The ball games were the culmination of months of religious fasting and preparation. The "playoffs" reduced the many participants to only the strongest, the fastest, and the bravest. For the winners of the final game, coming on the most sacred holiday, it would be an honor and privilege to be given to the gods at the pinnacle of their success. To consciously and humbly give oneself at the height of ones worldly accomplishment and spiritual potency—this sacrifice would surely result in ascension to the highest realms of Tollan, and please the highest gods.

Huxley refers to such a willful and willing self-sacrifice as self-abnegation. Ananda Coomaraswamy calls it "self-naughting" and offers a great deal of insight by anchoring the discussion to this idea's clear expression in Hindu and Vedic thought while constantly comparing it to theological statements and practices in Christianity and other major religions.

In his article "Self-Naughting," Coomaraswamy references the Satapatha Brahmana (III.8.1.2–3) to understand the inner meaning of self-sacrifice. In order to take possession of his "whole self" (sarvātmānan) the initiated one who sacrifices "is emptied out of himself . . . Man thus has two selves, lives or souls."[8] According to Coomaraswamy, the person who sacrifices and the sacrificial offering are one and the same, and fire rituals were the preferred rites used by the ancient Vedic and Hindu sages. The self-sacrifice (naughting or abnegation) must be a self-willed act. It must be something a person chooses to do, and herein lies a paradox, for choosing to relinquish control is a willful act, and thus associated with the ego's desire. The true basis of the self-sacrificial act is to assert our willingness to let go, be absorbed (or subsumed or translated) into the higher self, which is the Self of All. A great truth of Eastern religions is that the individual soul (Atman) is equivalent to the universal soul (Brahman).

The self-sacrifice is a willing plunge into the fire to disentangle karmic knots and is sustained by action through nonaction. This is another paradoxical teaching also found in *The Secret of the Golden Flower:* we dissolve the bonds of attachment to the results of our actions by *not being* the results that require the causes to continue existing. In other words, if the karmic results disappear (in the fire of self-sacrifice) there is no need for the karmic causes ever to have existed. Voilà! This is a bird's-eye view of the karmic Wheel of Becoming in which the fruit contains the seed of the future tree; the end result creates (or justifies) the causative agent. Alpha and Omega are one; the end is the beginning, and when we realize the end, we enter the timeless. And the end is complete re-absorption into the unmanifest divine ground.

Thus, seek the death and self-naughting that initiation into the perennial vision offers! Burn the dross of illusion in the fires of sacrifice, release your mortal attachments and spread the wings of the soul to fly upward and unite with the unmanifest root of the sacred tree of being!

8. Gnostic Eschatology. Page 13 of the Pyramid of Fire describes a universal conflagration, the final dissolution of the world by fire, which is quite similar to Gnostic eschatology. We can see that fire is a metaphor for the light of Tonatiuh, the divine ground that reclaims all manifestations, including individualized souls, which are like sparks of the primal Unity. And the process occurs in ever-repeating World Age cycles. Such a scenario is mentioned in Plato's *Timaeus*. In the same section of this book that relates the famous Atlantis myth, we read of an old Egyptian priest trying to convey a sense of the ancient teachings to Solon, who, as a visiting Greek, belongs to a culture that thinks "like children" and is not aware of the true age of the world. The priest recounts the Egyptian doctrine that the world has been destroyed by flood or fire many times in the past. The discussion moves to consider the Babylonian World Age tradition preserved by the sage Berossus (a near contemporary of Plato's). The Greek writer Seneca, mentioning Berossus in his *Quaestionis Naturales*, gives more details on the Babylonian World Age doctrine, saying that the world is alternately destroyed by flood or fire when the planets line up in

Capricorn or Cancer. Such a statement implies that global destructions occur at the two extreme poles of the Great Year of precession.*

Destruction of the world by fire (ekpyrosis) was a doctrine of the Stoic philosophers of Greece, who around the time that Hipparchus discovered precession (128 B.C.E.) believed that ekpyrosis occurs at the end of the current world order, at the end of the Great Year.† The later Gnostic teachings of Mani (in Manichaeism) applied this belief to a largely metaphysical system in which the final unredeemed particles in the fallen world of manifestation would be returned to the unmanifest godhead via a final conflagration, or ekpyrosis.[9]

Apart from literalist interpretations that expect the world to be burned to a cinder, the metaphysical idea implicit in ekpyrosis is that the eternal light of the divine ground occasionally flashes forth to incinerate illusion and free souls from the grip of physical matter. There is still room for a Gnostic dualism in this view, that of spirit and matter being irreconcilable opposites, but following the Pyramid of Fire, we have to remember that the transcendent divine ground pervades material existence and illuminates it from within (transcendence is inclusive). Thus, the incineration of every particle of matter is likened to a sublimation or transformation of gross material into its finest essence, thereby returning it to its original state of undifferentiated "light" within the unmanifest

---

* Rather than grouping all the planets in one sign, this scenario probably encodes (though fragmentarily) an astronomical alignment of one of the seasonal quarters—probably the spring equinox—with the cusp of Capricorn or Cancer. The spring equinox has long been used in the Old World as the tracking point for precession. Such a distinction is required because a mere grouping of planets does not involve precession, and yet precession is the cause of the Great Year. Popular stories derived from precessional mythology can be expected to result in distortions such as this. We see it, for example, in the popular 1960s song "The Age of Aquarius," in which a rare but random planetary alignment in a certain sign is thought to signal the dawn of a new precessional age. Such imagery works well for a song or a popular myth, but in actuality, an alignment caused by precession underlies all of these World Age shifts.

† Some scholars do not equate Plato's 36,000-year Great Year with precession (which involves 26,000 years), but an awareness of the shifting skies most certainly would have been rumored during the time that Plato lived through Babylonian astronomical knowledge. The indispensable book on this topic is Godefroid de Callataÿ, *Annus Platonicus: A Study of World Cycles in Greek, Latin and Arabic Sources* (Louvain-Paris: Institut Orientaliste and Peeters Press, 1996).

godhead. In this view the apparent opposition of matter and spirit is not a mutually exclusive opposition (as a pure Gnostic dualism would have it). Rather, this "opposition" is really the two poles of a continuum that defines a higher unity, in the same way that finitude rests within the bosom of infinity as one of infinity's potential states.

In Gnostic, Hebrew Scripture, and early Christian literature, the return of a soul to the divine source via a universal ekpyrosis is likened to a visionary ascent. This upward (and inward) journey attends the sublimation process noted earlier in *The Secret of the Golden Flower* and in Indian Kundalini yoga. *The Ascension of Isaiah* is an apocryphal first-century document that describes Isaiah's ascent to the throne of God. It is of a genre known as apocalypse literature, to which the testimonials of Ezekial, Daniel, and St. John (Revelation) also belong, because the macrocosmic end of the world is seen to be conceptually identical to the microcosmic (or personal) visionary ascent. Here again, the microcosm reflects the macrocosm.

The *Poimandres* is a Hermetic document that influenced Gnostic thought and yet was much like the earlier apocalypses of Daniel and Ezekial. Here we encounter that tumultuous milieu of the first and second centuries in which ideas were shared by both the Gnostic and early Christian movements—very profound metaphysical concepts that were eventually abandoned or edited out of official Church dogma. In the *Poimandres* we find a striking description, similar to the passage on page 13 of the Pyramid of Fire (13:10-19), of how the visionary's mortal coils are stripped away. According to the *Poimandres*, as the ascending visionary "thrusts upward through the Harmony" (the celestial spheres), he surrenders the power to grow and decay; his evil cunning is rendered powerless; deceit, concupiscence and arrogance are dissolved; impulsive acquisitiveness, appetite for wealth, and lying are all stripped away.[10] This is the soul's purification so that in its original state it can meet the unmanifest divine ground. Such a purification is often described as a burning away of the dross of individualized identity.

These descriptions in ascension literature are symbolic of an inward movement—a turning within for an inward (and upward) ascension. The profound association to be made here is that the personal visionary ascent maps onto apocalyptic descriptions of the universal conflagration (ekpyrosis) at the end of time.

Sacrifice, Sublimation, Ascension, and Apocalypse

Sublimation yoga and sacrifice are closely linked. In fact, sacrifice of outward attachments (and the consequent allegiance to a false ego identity that is reinforced by those attachments) is the prerequisite for sublimation, which involves the pointing inward of the seed energy of sexual reproduction. *Inward* thereafter transforms into *upward* as the seed energy is consumed within (burns) and rises higher through the inner spiritual physiology (the chakras).

The seed energy contains the latent power of creation—which the Pyramid of Fire identifies as being solar in origin—but when it is conserved and offered (burned) or sacrificed to a higher purpose, it transforms into light and illuminates a higher wisdom.* The sublimating, sacrificing seeker thereby becomes a Quetzalcoatl—an awakened seer who has activated the "two-headed serpent." He can act outwardly with the wisdom of an awakened transcendent viewpoint.

The sublimation of creative energy that is possible through sacrifice is equivalent to what in Hindu parlance is called a Kundalini awakening. As we have already sketched, in Hebrew Scripture and Gnostic visionary literature such an awakening experience is characterized as an ascension. Often in this apocalypse literature—in the Gnostic *Poimandres,* for example—the ascension is attended by the stripping away of the seeker's false self-identifications and attachments. This Gnostic doctrine of the anagogical (upward-leading) journey has a precedent in the Sumerian "descent" of Inanna, who must disrobe at each successive level until she stands naked before the Annunaki judges in the deepest level of the Underworld. (In this instance Inanna's "descent" is equivalent to the

---

* It should be mentioned that there is a yoga of self-actualization intended for women. However, it is by nature a very different path, for men seek to transcend phenomena, whereas women by nature seek to wear phenomena as ornaments—that is to say, to embody the energies of the universe. One form of yoga for women teaches how to embody (channel or "download") the goddess energies of evolutionary transmutation through sacred dance. See Rose, 2001 and 2003.

Gnostic "ascent." In the *Poimandres* the soul's ascent is the reversal of the process by which the soul descends or falls into material incarnation.) And of course, the Pyramid of Fire likewise requires the discarding of mortal attachments (the "clothes" of individualized identity) as shown in the following excerpt (13:11–19):

> Now Cihuacóatl, Ehécatl, Chalciuhtlicue, and Xiuhtecuhtli
> incendiate the *four elements*.
> The seven planetary gods throw my constituent parts into
> the fire:
> Tlaltecuhtli, my *bones*
> Metztli, my *viscera*
> Paynal, my *members*
> Itzpapálotl, my sweet *flesh*
> Huitzilopochtli adds my *passion*
> Tezcatlipoca, my *sorrow*
> Mixcóatl, my fragile *mind*.

Both sacrifice and sublimation lead to the visionary ascent, which, as we have seen, is memorialized in the apocalypse literature of various religious traditions that were in vogue in the Near East just after the Crucifixion. But why is such ascent literature characterized as "apocalyptic"? The reason is that the visionary ascends to a realm that transcends the temporal flow. This ascent provides a direct ecstatic immersion in the eternal wisdom (the *Sophia perennis*) at the root and source of all phenomenal manifestation. This source is the "nowhere" place that endures throughout all the vicissitudes of World Ages coming and going. It is that which remains after the Apocalypse (the "unveiling") strips away all separating distinctions and dissolves all manifestations into the divine ground from which they came. It is a glimpse of the end of time and the end of the world.

This end place is also the place of origin. These ideas are recognized by Dead Sea Scroll scholars as a paradigm called *realized eschatology*. At the hermitage of Qumran—the society that followed a secret teaching of Jesus and whose documents, the Nag Hammadi library, were unearthed in the 1940s—the quest for afterlife salvation was irrelevant. They were more concerned with creating a society of people based upon *practicing* immersion in the transcendent divine ground. The direct experience of the godhead was seen to be a nectar useful for creating an authentic spiritually based paradigm on Earth. They had realized their eschatology—they knew how to access the transcendent divine ground and could do so on a regular basis. In other words, they had made manifest the New Jerusalem or Heavenly Kingdom that the New Testament (fixated upon linear time concepts) puts off until after the Apocalypse and Last Judgment.* What they sought to manifest on Earth was the *eschaton,* the end state.[11]

Thus, the personal visionary ascent is a death-to-ego initiation into gnostic (direct) experience of the transcendent divine ground, leading to the second birth that begins a new spiritualized existence (even while still on Earth). This is actually what it means to be truly human or, said another way, such a state is the fully actualized potential of all human beings—the immediate awareness of true nature unconditioned by artificial distinctions and the attachment to becoming. That true nature is eternal and infinite. The ecstatic exaltation of immersion in such a state is what Seyyed Hossein Nasr described in his book *Knowledge and the Sacred,* implying that all true knowledge comes from an ecstatic connection with (experience of) the transcendent.[12] Such an experience is timeless, and even if not sustained, it imprints the seeker with a conviction that his true nature is eternal and infinite. He has been to the end of the world; he has seen the apocalypse; he has been burned (initiated, purified) in the fires of a universal ekpyrosis that all manifested beings will eventually undergo.

According to the Pyramid of Fire, we can go willingly to our destiny or resist it until what appear to be the demonic minions of death's destiny strip away the ego-illusion. We may witness the difficult struggle of resisting dissolution as a loved one dies, the irony (and possibility) of choice while being catapulted through a process beyond human control. Without presuming to peer beyond the veil of death, it is possible to

---

* Such historical locating of the end of time is an absurdity from the higher viewpoint of realized eschatology (see Henry Corbin's *Temple and Contemplation*). Realized eschatology is criticized as a dangerous heresy in mainstream theological discourse today.

observe that in the death process, we can let go and thereby smooth the experience of dissolution, or we can hold on, resist the inevitable, and thereby oblige death to take all by force.

Such a "pay the piper" imperative may seem harsh, but it does speak a truth—that of free will within the limits of karma. Much has been written about the death process, and many believe that 2012 (the end of the Mayan calendar) is about the end of the world. Visionary philosopher Terence McKenna often emphasized in public addresses that the psychedelic state of consciousness was something to be experienced; it isn't a doctrine or set of beliefs in some culturally relative system. It is, first and foremost—and above all—an experience. The overly flogged "end of the world" in 2012 should be viewed in a similar vein. Let's all experience the end of the world before we pass judgment on it. It would be difficult to talk about the end of time and the end of the world unless it was with someone who had been there.

The end of the world is cognate with (or equivalent to) the visionary ascent and the death/rebirth initiation. This inner experience casts us out of the flow of mundane time to glimpse the realm beyond time, beyond the end of time, which is not to be identified with any point on the historical continuum but is found when the consciousness shifts to a vertical movement or ascent *above* the horizontal plane of historical flow. Thus, what 2012 is about (as the end-of-time archetype) is an experience of no time, an experience of the perspective achieved when time is transcended (ended). The root of time is the timeless. That experience, as we find it reflected in the Gnostic *Poimandres,* can certainly be documented and added to the corpus of testimonials, but even though the human reflex is to make a model, no resulting dogmas should define the experience for others.

Apocalypse literature intriguingly points the way to an experience that can be achieved at any point within the historical continuum, and according to the Nahuatl philosophers (and possibly the eschaton seers of Qumran themselves) is best achieved with sacred plants, flower and song combined with self-sacrifice and commitment to nonattachment. In fact, self-sacrifice and nonattachment are the teachings that Huxley observes in all perennial philosophies as the means to achieve the

Fig. 6.1. The visionary initiate with eyes wide open

ultimate purpose of human life: the soul's reunion with the higher divine self.[13]

And so the actual temporal location of the end-time is a moot question, for the emphasis in the Pyramid of Fire is on personal transcendence and ascent to "the end of time." A ritual or symbolic death—an ecstatic visionary experience of the after-death state, the state that is above or beyond (transcendent to) the linear flow of time—has always been a central feature of initiation rituals. What this means is obvious but not often thought about clearly: *Many initiates and spiritual seekers have already been to the end of time*, and to try to locate "the end of time" somewhere within the temporal flow simply misses the point. Identifying the end-time date is certainly useful for anchoring a World Age doctrine or as something upon which to hang prophetic utterances, but the transcendental metaphysics of ascension do not require that anyone must wait until a future time to experience the timeless.

APPENDIX 1

Quetzalcoatl's Ascension

The vision of Venus rising as morning star, powerful and accessible to people even today, is at the core of an important Aztec teaching. It is the metaphor of the spirit breaking free from the bonds of ego. The cycles of the stars and planets mirror perfectly the cycles of human culture. Themes and patterns repeat themselves on various levels of reality; for example, the sun sets in the western sky and, likewise, as cultures evolve, the spirit descends into matter to animate, be molded by, and become lost in it. And the dark night of the soul ensues. But the occluded souls know the "sun" is down there somewhere, untouched by the dark fact that they can no longer see their origin. And when the time comes, the source emerges to enlighten the body of the earth, and green growing things rejoice.

Venus plays an important part in the story of Quetzalcoatl, the Plumed Serpent. Here again, the Aztecs have seen in the complexities of astronomical cycles the journey of the soul toward enlightenment. In this sense "myth" is not a time-worn legend to be considered the fantasy of a dead people. The meaning behind the legend of Quetzalcoatl's death and rebirth is a meaning shared by cultures all around the world.

The Tibetan Book of the Dead tells of the soul's journey through the Underworld after death. The soul experiences various benevolent and frightful deities that we are encouraged to remember as mere projections of the mind. The goal is to reach the highest Bardo, or plane of consciousness, where we are liberated from the illusory creations of the mind, where we experience pure awareness. If we are unable to transcend mind-created desires, we swoon into unconsciousness to be reborn on Earth. During the soul's new incarnation on Earth, it is hoped that we will achieve a deeper understanding of the nature of reality.

Frank Waters, in his book *Mexico Mystique*, commented on the story of Quetzalcoatl and found it is reflected in the movement of Venus through the sky. It symbolizes the redemption of the spirit after a downfall and suggests that a fall, or the loss of consciousness into matter, is part of the great cycles of time. Inevitably we arrive at an era of regeneration and rebirth of the spirit—the end of an age—which for the Maya is December 21, 2012 C.E. Here is a brief recounting of the myth of Quetzalcoatl, paraphrased from the *Anales de Cuauhtitlan*.

As the ruler of the City of the Gods established after the creation of the Fifth Sun, Quetzalcoatl was good, wise, and chaste. Then his old heavenly rival and dual antithesis, Tezcatlipoca, contrived his downfall. Tezcatlipoca brought him a mirror and said to him, "Ce Acatl Quetzalcoatl, I greet thee and come to give thee thy body."

Quetzalcoatl, conscious of his divine origin, was perplexed. "My body? What is this concerning my body? Let me see."

And seeing his earthly body for the first time reflected in the mirror, he was very frightened.

Tezcatlipoca then tempted him with a drink of pulque. Quelzatcoatl refused.

"Just taste it," insisted Tezcatlipoca.

Quetzalcoatl tasted it with his little finger and found it to be good. So he took a drink. He took four drinks and a fifth, after which he called for his sister, Xochiquetzal, goddess of love and beauty. She too drank the pulque and in the end they slept together.

Upon awakening, Quetzalcoatl realized he had been induced to become drunk, forget his chastity, and commit incest. "Woe is me!" he wailed, singing a sad song of departure. "Acolytes, this is it. I shall go away. Have a stone box made for me."

A stone coffin was made at once. In it Quetzalcoatl immured himself for four days. He then disposed of all his material riches, and went to *la orilla celeste del agua divina*, the shore of the divine sea. During his pilgrimage, necromancers kept asking him, "Why have you left your people? Where are you going?"

"I go to Tlillan Tlapallan. The sun is calling me."

Arriving at the seacoast, he put on his feathers and mask and built a great fire. Then he cast himself into the flames. When he burned, all the rare birds gathered to watch his ashes rise. And then eight days later his heart rose like a flaming star.

After his mortal manifestation died in the funeral pyre, Quetzalcoatl went underground to Mictlan, the Land of the Dead. He was accompanied by his twin or double, Xolotl, who took the shape of a dog. From Mictlantecuhtli, the Lord of the Dead, he took the bones of a man and a woman and escaped after many trials. He then sprinkled the bones with his own blood, thus redeeming them so that they could inhabit the earth.

Four days more he spent making arrows and on the eighth day he made his ascent, being transformed into the Lord of the Dawn, the morning star. Thereafter, as the planet Venus he astronomically repeats his ritual journey, first appearing in the western sky as the evening star, disappearing underground, and then reappearing in the eastern sky as the morning star to unite with the rising sun.[1]

What is the transcendental meaning of this myth? It expresses the universal theme of sin and redemption, of death and resurrection, the transfiguration of human into God. But if Quetzalcoatl, one of the four sons of the supreme creator, Ometeotl, was already divine, how could he have succumbed to mortal sin? Simply because the myth enunciates the principle of all creation: the incarnation of divine light, purity, and spirituality into gross matter, followed by the agonizing redemption of matter by spirituality. This is the immortal theme of all religions: *the movement of the unconscious into consciousness*. The self-illumination of consciousness *by* consciousness, the source of all true transformation.

The priest-astronomers of the Nahuas and Mayans devoted special attention to the phases of the planet Venus. A study of the Mayan Dresden Codex shows that the synodical period of Venus was estimated at 584 days (583.92, by modern calculations). The synodical period refers to the time it takes for Venus to cycle around and appear as the morning star once again. While the time Venus takes to circle the sun is roughly 225 days, the movement of Earth itself necessitates adding time for Venus to "catch up" to its former observed location. Earth, of course, takes 365.242 days to revolve once around the sun, which the Maya approximated as 365 days. And the synodical period of Venus is 584 days. The relationship between the numbers 365 and 584 is 5 to 8—the ratio between the fifth and eighth tones in a musical scale. The 260-day Mayan Sacred Calendar incorporates these two cycles, along with the lunar eclipse cycle and the phases of the moon, and, amazingly, is a harmonic sub-unit of the great 26,000-year cycle of the precession of the equinoxes. The sacred number 260 is the key to Mesoamerican time philosophy.

Each synodical revolution of Venus was observed to consist of four phases. The first phase is the eight-day period when Venus crosses in front of the sun. This is called inferior conjunction. The first annual predawn appearance of Venus (west of the rising sun) is called its heliacal rising. During this early-morning viewing period Venus is fantastically brilliant because of its proximity to Earth. As the days of this second phase advance, Venus progresses farther away from Earth, becoming visible as a morning star for a longer period each day. At its greatest "western elongation" from the Sun, Venus rises three hours ahead of it, then as the weeks progress, it closes in on the Sun and disappears behind the glare of the Sun for about eight weeks. This is superior conjunction, phase three. As this period of invisibility ends, Venus appears briefly in the western sky right after sunset, and as the days of phase four progress, is eventually visible for as much as three hours after sunset. This is the point of maximum eastern elongation, after which Venus closes in on the Sun very quickly to repeat the cycle in inferior conjunction.

The eight days of inferior conjunction represent the time that Quetzalcoatl spends in the Underworld, the Land of the Dead, after which he is redeemed and rises triumphant as the morning star.

Nahuatl
Pronunciation Guide

Centéotl: Sen-**TAY**-otl

Centzon Mimixcoa: Sent-zon Mee-**MEESH**-kowah

Centzonhuitznáuac: Sent-zon-weets-**NOW**-ok

Chalchiuhtlicue: Chal-chee-**OOHT**-lee-kway

Chicomecoatl: Cheeko-may-**CO**-atl

Cauhlacan: Kowlah-**KAN**

Cihuacóatl: Seehwah-**CO**-atl

Coatlicue: Ko-**WATT**-lee-kway

Coyolxauhqui: Koy-yol-**SHAUW**-kwee (*shauw* rhymes with *how*)

Ehécatl: Ay-**HAY**-catl

Huitzilopochtli: Hoo-weet-zeeloh-**POACH**-tlee

Itzlacoliuqui: Eets-lah-kohlee-**OOH**-kwee

Itzli: **EETS**-lee

Itzpapálotl: Eets-pah-**PAH**-loattle

Ixcuina: Eesh-**KWEE**-nah

Metztli: Mets-tlee

Mictecacíhuatl: Mik-tay-kah-**SEE**-hwatl

Mictlantecuhtli: Mik-tlan-tay-**KOO**-tlee

Mixcóatl: Mesh-**KOH**-atl

Ometecuhtli: Oh-may-tay-koo-tli

Paynal: Pay-**NAHL**

Quetzalcoatl: Keht-zahl-**koh**-atl (also = Kwet-zahl-**KOH**-atl)

Tecciztécatl: Tek-seez-**TAY**-cottle

Teoyaomiqui: Tay-oh-yow-**MEE**-kwee

Tezcatlipoca: Tez-cot-lee-po-ka

Tlahuizcalpantecuhtli: Tlah-**HWEEZ**-kal-**PON**-tay-koo-tlee

Tlaloc: Tlah-loke (*loke* rhymes with *broke*)

Tlaltecuhtli: Tlahl-tay-**KOO**-tlee

Tlamatinime: Tlah-mah-**TEE**-nee-may

Tlazolteotl: Tlah-zol-**tay**-otl

Tloque Nahuaque: Tlow-kay Nah-**HWOK**-ay

Tonacacíhuatl: Tone-ah-kah-**SEE**-hwatl

Tonacatecuhtli: Tone-ah-kah-tay-**KOO**-tlee

Tonalpohualli: Tone-ahl-poh-**WOLL**-ee (*ahl* rhymes with *doll*)

Tonatiuh: Tone-ah-tee-oo (*oo* rhymes with *shoe*)

Tzitzímime: Tsee-**TSEE**-mee-may

Xipe Totec: **SHEEP**-pay **TOE**-tek (*Toe* rhymes with *grow*)

Xiuhtecuhtli: Shee-ooht-tay-**KOO**-tlee

Xochipilli: Zoe-chee-**PEE**-lee

Xochiquetzal: Zoe-chee-**KET**-zahl

A Glossary of Aztec Gods and Goddesses

The following is a glossary Barbara Matz made for herself so that she could keep at hand the meanings of the various Aztec gods and goddesses as she worked to get at the inner truths contained in the Pyramid of Fire.

Centzon Mimixcoa: four hundred to the north

Centzonhuitznáuac: four hundred to the south

Chalchiuhtlicue: She of the Jeweled Gown; governs passive, feminine matter, water; Goddess of Terrestrial Waters

Cihuacóatl: the Woman Serpent; governs matter that is inert, current of all forces, earth; the seventh serpent, Goddess of Corn; governs the windy season, autumn

Centéotl: God of Corn

Coatl: man's own serpent, the energy of Tonatiuh

Coatlicue: dressed with serpents

Coyolxauhqui: sister of Metztli; governs the Moon

Ehécatl: God of the Wind, governs impartial, unifying, mediating matter and wind

Huitzilopochtli: the Hummingbird Magician; Mars; governs the fight and the war in men

Itzlacoliuhqui: Obsidian Knife; Goddess of Sacrifice

Itzpapálotl: Obsidian Butterfly, Venus; governs the new growth and the death and rebirth of creatures

Metztli: the Moon

Mictecacíhuatl: Lady of Death

Mictlantecuhtli: Lord of Death

Mixcóatl: the Cloud Serpent; Saturn

Ometecuhtli: Lord of Duality

Paynal: the Speedy Runner, Mercury; governs the movement and dance of men

Quetzalcoatl: Venus; the Plumed Serpent, the link between gods and men; Lord of our Sustainment; governs the new growth and the death and rebirth of the souls of men

Tecciztécatl: He of the Marine Conch; governs the Moon

Teoyaomiqui: Lord of the Dead Warrior

Tezcatlipoca: Smoking Mirror; Jupiter; Falcon, Herald of the Gods

Tlahuizcalpantecuhtli: Lord of Morning

Tlaloc: He Who Forms Germination; governs the humid season, summer; God of Celestial Water

Tlaltecuhtli: Lord of our Planet, the Earth

Tlazolteotl: Mother Earth in her Ixcuina disguise as consumer of waste

Tloque Nahuaque: Lord of the Intimate Vicinity; Universal Spirit; the Absolute

Tonacacíhuatl: Lady of Our Sustainment

Tonacatecuhtli: Lord of Our Sustainment; father of all the gods; creator of all the cosmoses and all the galaxies

Tonalpohualli: Aztec 260-day calendar that governs the life of man

Tonatiuh: Lord of our Solar System, giver of life to all; the Sun

Tzitzímime: giants that descend from the sky above our galaxy

Xipe Totec: the Skinned One; governs the ardent season, spring

Xiuhtecuhtli: Lord of the Year, governs active, masculine matter, fire; Lord of Fire

Xochipilli: Flourished Prince

Xochiquetzal: Flourished Plume; nature; Goddess of All That Lives, Grows, Flowers, and is Engendered

Resources

Marty Matz's Poetry and Interviews

"The Alchemist's Song"
www.taolodge.com.tw/bigsmoke
Peter Lee's book *The Big Smoke: The Chinese Art and Craft of Opium* contains Marty's poem "The Alchemist's Song." The two were friends in Thailand, and the book can be ordered here.

East Village Poetry Scene
www.EastVillagePoetry.com
This Web site, created by Anne Lombardo Ardolina, contains a recollection of Marty and news about goings-on in the East Village poetry scene.

Fang Records
www.FangRecords.com
Marty's two poetry CDs—*A Sky of Fractured Feathers* (2000) and *Pipe Dreams* (2003), which include the accompaniment of Chris Rael and Church of Betty—can be ordered here.

Goodie Magazine
197 Seventh Ave., 4C, New York, NY 10011
www.Goodie.org
Issue no. 6, featuring an interview with Marty by Romy Ashby, can be found here.

The Official Marty Matz Web Site
www.Alignment2012.com/pipedreams.html
(soon to be relocated to www.MartyMatz.com)
Contains links to recollections of and eulogies for Marty, excerpts from
his writings, CDs, and collections of his poetry, including the updated
edition of *Pipe Dreams.*

Panther Books
197 Seventh Ave., 4C, New York, NY 10011
www.goodie.org/panther/panther.html
In the Seasons of My Eye: Selected works of Marty Matz can be ordered here.

Mesoamerican Cosmology and Calendar Systems

Aztec Calendars
www.resonateview.org
This Web site, created by Yari Jeada, contains writing on Aztec calendars
and Toltec Nagualism.

John Major Jenkins's Web Site
www.Alignment2012.com
This site features upcoming speaking engagements, articles, and excerpts
from his books on Mesoamerican cosmology and metaphysics.

One Reed Publications:
www.onereed.com
Bruce Scofield's books and Web site provide insight into Aztec calendars
and astrology.

Aztec Poetry and Aztec-Influenced Art

Aztec Tlamatinime Poetry
www.red-coral.net/Hungry.html
English translations of the poetry and Flower Songs of the Aztec tlamatinime Hungry Coyote (Nezahual coyotl) can be found here.

Stevon Lucero
www.StevonLucero.com
This visionary artist's original prints and oil paintings incorporate Neo-
Pre-Columbian style and Meta-Realism, a philosophy inspired by Mayan
and Aztec motifs. His work can be ordered here.

Notes

Introduction: Nahuatl Poetry and Metaphysics

1. See Miguel León-Portilla, *Aztec Thought and Culture: A Study of the Ancient Nahuatl Mind* (Norman: University of Oklahoma Press, 1963).
2. Translation from León-Portilla, *Aztec Thought and Culture*, 72.
3. Ibid., 74–75.
4. Juan D. García Bacca, "Comentarios a La Esencia de la Poesía de Heidegger," *Revista Nacional de Cultura*, no. 112–13 (1955): 226.
5. Jacques Soustelle, *La Vie Quotidienne de Aztèques à la Veille de la Conquête Espagnole* (Paris: Librairie Hachtte, 1955), 275.

Chapter 1: Marty Matz and the Lost Codex

1. Marty Matz, quoted in Romy Ashby, *Goodie Magazine*, no. 6, 2000.
2. In Laki Vazakas, "Remembering Marty Matz," *Polarity eMagazine*, 2000. www.poembeat.com/current/laki_vazakas.html.
3. Roger Richards, "Marty Matz: Falstaff in Leather Stetson and Vest," www.EastVillagePoetry.com, 2002.
4. "I Know Where Rainbows Go to Die," in Marty Matz, *Time Waits: Selected Poems 1956–1986*, San Francisco: JMF Publishing, 1987. Barbara Matz Alexander designed the second edition of this collection, released in 1994, as well as the beautiful first edition of Marty's *Pipe Dreams* (self-published in 1989).
5. From Matz, "Under the Influence of Mozart," *Time Waits*.
6. In Vazakas, "Remembering Marty Matz."
7. See Peter Lee's book *The Big Smoke: The Chinese Art and Craft of Opium* (Thailand: Lamplight Books, 1999), www.taolodge.com.tw/

bigsmoke. The Marty Matz official Web site is www.Alignment 2012.com/pipedreams.html.

8. Marty's CDs can be purchased at Fang Records, www.fangrecords. com.

9. John B. Glass, "A Survey of Native Middle American Pictorial Manuscripts," in *The Handbook of Middle American Indians,* vol. 14, part 3, ed. Howard Cline (Austin: University of Texas Press, 1975), 73; John B. Glass and Donald Roberston, "A Census of Native Middle American Pictorial Manuscripts," in *The Handbook of Middle American Indians,* vol. 14, part 3, ed. Howard Cline (Austin: University of Texas Press, 1975), 185.

10. John Kolemainen, *Epic of the North: The Story of Finland's Kalevala* (New York Mills, Minn.: Northwestern Press, 1973), 22–30.

11. Miguel León-Portilla, *Aztec Thought and Culture: A Study of the Ancient Nahuatl Mind* (Norman: University of Oklahoma Press, 1963).

12. See Dennis Tedlock, trans., *The Popol Vuh: The Definitive Edition of the Mayan Book of the Dawn of Life and the Glories of Gods and Kings* (New York: Simon and Schuster, 1996).

13. J. J. Hurtak, *The Keys of Enoch* (Los Gatos, Calif.: The Academy for Future Science, 1977). For Book of Mormon/Cerro Rabon connections, see the "Cave" section of The Academy Web site: "Sealed Records of Mexico" at www.nebulus.org/academy/cave/plcave6.html; cave library of Cumorah Hill at www.nebulus.org/academy/ cave/plcave7.html (a picture of Cerro Rabon can be found here); and www.nebulus.org/academy/cave/cvpic4.html, where a map of the area of Cerro Rabon can be found.

Chapter 3: *The Pyramid of Fire: A Novella*

1. Antonio de Herrera y Tordesillas, *Historia de las Indias Occidentales,* Decada iv, Lib. viii, cap. 4 (Madrid: Libreria del la Publicidad, 1854), English translation in Daniel Brinton, "Nagualism: A Study in Native American Folk-lore and History," *Proceedings of the American Philosophical Society* 33 (1894): 4–5.

2. Francisco Antonio de Fuentes y Guzman, *Historia de Guatemala o Recordacion Florida,* vol. 2 (Madrid: L Navarro, 1882–1883), 44.

English translation in Brinton, *Nagualism: A Study in Native American Folk-lore and History*, 23.

3. John Major Jenkins, *Maya Cosmogenesis 2012*, chapters 6–8.

4. See "Self Naughting" and "Self Sacrifice" in Ananda Coomaraswamy, *Coomaraswamy: Metaphysics,* ed. Roger Lipsey (Princeton, N.J.: Princeton University Press, 1977).

5. Friberg, *The Kalevala: Epic of the Finnish People*, Runo 17:507-510.

Chapter 4: The Text

1. Frances Karttunen, *An Analytical Dictionary of Nahuatl* (Austin: University of Texas Press, 1983).

Chapter 5: Commentary

1. Henry Nicholson, "Religion in Pre-Hispanic Central Mexico," in *The Handbook of Middle American Indians,* vol. 10 (Austin: University of Texas Press, 1971). See also Gordon Ekholm and John Glass, "Archaeology of Northern Mesoamerica," in *The Handbook of Middle American Indians,* vol. 10 (Austin: University of Texas Press, 1971).

2. Bruce Scofield, *Signs of Time: An Introduction to Mesoamerican Astrology* (Amherst, Mass.: One Reed Publications, 1994), 81–89.

3. P. D. Ouspensky, *In Search of the Miraculous: Fragments of an Unknown Teaching* (London: HBJ Publishers, 1949), 77.

4. Ibid., 79.

5. Ibid., 82–86, 137–40, 167–69.

6. Ibid., 85, 139, 305.

7. Dennis Tedlock, *Breath on the Mirror: Mythic Voices and Visions of the Living Maya* (San Francisco: Harper San Francisco, 1993).

8. For more on how the three sacred science principles manifest in Mayan time philosophy, see my book *Mayan Sacred Science* (Boulder, Colo.: Four Ahau Press, 1994).

9. Tony Shearer, *Lord of the Dawn: Quetzalcoatl and the Tree of Life* (Healdsburg, Calif.: Naturegraph, 1971), 184. See also Shearer, *Beneath the Moon and Under the Sun* (Albuquerque, N.M.: Sun Publishing, 1975).

10. See Robert Carlsen and Martín Prechtel, "Weaving and Cosmos amongst the Tzutujil Maya of Guatemala," in *Res* 15 (1988) and "The Flowering of the Dead: An Interpretation of Highland Maya Culture," in *Man* 26 (1990).

11. For my theory regarding the precessional astronomy embedded in the New Fire/Calendar Round eschatology, see my book *Maya Cosmogenesis 2012* (Rochester, Vt.: Bear and Company, 1998), chapters 6–8.

12. Wilhelm, *The Secret of the Golden Flower,* trans. C. F. Baynes, commentary by Carl Jung (New York: Harcourt, Brace, Jovanovich, 1962).

13. See Jenkins, *Maya Cosmogenesis 2012*, 30–41.

14. These terms come from the work of Ananda Coomaraswamy in "The Sundoor and Related Motifs," Roger Lipsey, ed.; *Coomaraswamy: Traditional Art and Symbolism* (Princeton, N.J.: Princeton University Press, 1977).

15. From Jenkins, *Metaphysical Speculations: Collected Poetry, 1982–1998* (Boulder, Colo.: Four Ahau Press, 1998).

16. Mary Ellen Miller and Karl Taube, *The Gods and Symbols of Ancient Mexico and the Maya: An Illustrated Dictionary of Mesoamerican Religion* (New York: Thames and Hudson, 1993), 141.

17. Neil Asher Silberman, *Heavenly Powers: Unraveling the Secret History of the Kabbalah* (Edison, N.J.: Castle Books, 2000), 115–16.

18. Dennis Tedlock, trans., *The Popol Vuh: The Definitive Edition of the Mayan Book of the Dawn of Life and the Glories of Gods and Kings* (New York, Simon and Schuster, 1996), 334, 358.

19. Seyyed Hossein Nasr, *Knowledge and the Sacred* (Albany: State University of New York Press, 1989), 280–328. Also listen online to Nasr's lecture "Knowledge and the Sacred" at www.serious seekers.com.

20. Derek Walters, *Fortune-Telling by Mah Jongg: A Practical Guide to Divination Using the Ancient Chinese Game of Mah Jongg* (Wellingborough, England: Aquarian Press, 1987), 29–30.

21. See, for example, Henry Nicholson, "Religion in Pre-Hispanic Central Mexico," in *The Handbook of Middle American Indians,* vol.

10 (Austin: University of Texas Press, 1971), Miguel León-Portilla, *Aztec Thought and Culture: A Study of the Ancient Nahuatl Mind* (Norman: University of Oklahoma Press, 1963), Burr Cartwright Brundage, *The Fifth Sun: Aztec Gods, Aztec World* (Austin: University of Texas Press, 1979), all citing codices Borgia, Borbonicus, and Nuttall.

22. See Greenway's introduction to Bernardino de Sahagún, *A History of Ancient Mexico: The Religion and Ceremonies of the Aztec Indians* (Glorieta, N. M.: Rio Grande Press, 1976), 32.

23. Ibid., 32–34.

Chapter 6: Perennial and Gnostic Parallels to the Pyramid of Fire

1. Aldous Huxley, from the introduction to Swami Prabhavananda and Christopher Isherwood, *The Song of God, Bhagavad Gita* (New York: New American Library, 1954), 13.

2. See my books *Tzolkin: Visionary Perspectives and Calendar Studies* and *7 Wind: A Quiché Maya Calendar for 1993* online at www.Alignment2012.com. Also see Barbara Tedlock, *Time and the Highland Maya* (Albuquerque: University of New Mexico Press, 1982).

3. Jenkins, *Maya Cosmogenesis 2012* (Rochester, Vt.: Bear and Company, 1998), chapters 6–9.

4. See Gordon Brotherston, "The Year 3113 B.C. and the Fifth Sun of Mesoamerica: An Orthodox Reading of the Tepexic Annals," in *Calendars of Mesoamerica and Peru*, ed. Anthony F. Aveni and Gordon Brotherston (Oxford: B.A.R. International Series 174, 1983) and *The Book of the Fourth World: Reading the Native Americans through Their Literature* (Cambridge: Cambridge University Press, 1992), and Eva Hunt, *The Transformation of the Hummingbird: Cultural Roots of a Zinacantecan Mythical Poem* (Ithaca, N.Y.: Cornell University Press, 1977). Appendix 2 in *Maya Cosmogenesis 2012* surveys the academic literature on this question in great detail.

5. This insight came after reading Martín Prechtel's articles and meeting him in early 1993. See Robert Carlsen and Martín Prechtel, "Weaving

and Cosmos amongst the Tzutujil Maya of Guatemala," in *Res* 15 (1988), and "The Flowering of the Dead: An Interpretation of Highland Maya Culture," in *Man* 26 (1990).

6. See Pekka Ervast, *The Key to the Kalevala* (Nevada City, Calif.: Blue Dolphin Publishing, 1999).
7. For more Nahuatl poetry, see the "Hungry Coyote" Web site: www.red-coral.net/Hungry.html
8. See Coomaraswamy, "Self-Naughting," in *Coomaraswamy: Metaphysics,* ed. Roger Lipsey (Princeton, N.J.: Princeton University Press, 1977), 93.
9. See Hans Jonas, *The Gnostic Religion: The Message of the Alien God and the Beginnings of Christianity,* 2nd ed. (Boston: Beacon Press, 1991), 206–36.
10. Ibid., 153.
11. The term *eschaton* was used by Henry Corbin in his 1974 Eranos lecture entitled, "L'Imago Templi face aux Normes Profanes," translated and published in his *Temple and Contemplation* (London: KPI Limited, 1986).
12. Seyyed Hossein Nasr, Islamic scholar and Traditionalist philosopher, explained this principle clearly in his book *Knowledge and the Sacred* (Albany: State University of new York Press, 1974), 280–328.
13. Aldous Huxley, from the introduction to Prabhavananda and Isherwood, *The Song of God, Bhagavad Gita,* 13.

Appendix 1: Quetzalcoatl's Ascension

1. John Major Jenkins, *Journey to the Mayan Underworld* (Boulder, Colo.: Four Ahau Press, 1989), 10–11.

Bibliography

Ambrose, Joe. *Chelsea Hotel, Manhattan.* New York: Codex Books, 2003.

Anales de Cuauhtitlan. See Waters, 1975.

Ashby, Romy. "Martin Matz." *Goodie Magazine,* no. 6, 2000.

Auger, Helen. *Zapotec.* New York: Dolphin Books, 1954.

Bernbaum, Edwin. *The Way to Shambhala.* New York: Anchor Books, 1980.

Boone, Elizabeth. *The Codex Magliabechiano and the Lost Prototype of the Magliabechiano Group.* Berkeley, Calif.: University of California Press, 1983.

Brinton, Daniel. "Nagualism: A Study in Native American Folk-lore and History." *Proceedings of the American Philosophical Society,* vol. 33, 1894.

Brotherston, Gordon. "The Year 3113 B.C. and the Fifth Sun of Mesoamerica: An Orthodox Reading of the Tepexic Annals." In *Calendars of Mesoamerica and Peru.* Edited by Anthony F. Aveni and Gordon Brotherston. Oxford: B.A.R. International Series 174, 1983.

———. *The Book of the Fourth World: Reading the Native Americans through Their Literature.* Cambridge: Cambridge University Press, 1992.

Brundage, Burr Cartwright. *The Fifth Sun: Aztec Gods, Aztec World.* Austin: University of Texas Press, 1979.

de Callataÿ, Godefroid. *Annus Platonicus: A Study of World Cycles in Greek, Latin and Arabic Sources.* Louvain-Paris: Institut Orientaliste and Peeters Press, 1996.

Carlsen, Robert S., and Martín Prechtel. "Weaving and Cosmos amongst the Tzutujil Maya of Guatemala." In *Res* 15 (1988): 122–32.

———. "The Flowering of the Dead: An Interpretation of Highland Maya Culture." In *Man* 26 (1990): 23–42.

Cline, Howard. *Guide to Ethohistorical Sources: The Handbook of Middle American Indians,* vols. 12–15. Austin: University of Texas Press, 1972–1975.

Codex Borbonicus. Commentary by Karl Nowotny, description by Jacqueline de Durand-Forest. Graz, Germany: Verlagsanstalt Akademische Druck-u, 1974.

Codex Borgia. A Full-Color Restoration of the Ancient Mexican Manuscript. Edited by Gisele Díaz and Alan Rodgers. New York: Dover Publications, 1993.

Codex Nuttall. A Picture Manuscript From Ancient Mexico. Edited by Zelia Nuttall, introduction by Arthur G. Miller. New York: Dover Publications, 1975.

Coomaraswamy, Ananda. *Coomaraswamy: Traditional Art and Symbolism.* Edited by Roger Lipsey. Princeton, N.J.: Princeton University Press, 1977.

———. *Coomaraswamy: Metaphysics.* Edited by Roger Lipsey, Princeton, N.J.: Princeton University Press, 1977.

Corbin, Henry. *Temple and Contemplation.* London: KPI Limited, 1986.

Ekholm, Gordon, and John B. Glass. "Archaeology of Northern Mesoamerica." In *The Handbook of the Middle American Indians,* vol. 10. Austin: University of Texas Press, 1971.

Ervast, Pekka. *The Key to the Kalevala.* Nevada City, Calif.: Blue Dolphin Publishing, 1999.

Friberg, Eino. *The Kalevala: Epic of the Finnish People.* Helsinki, Finland: Otava Publishing, 1988.

de Fuentes y Guzman, Francisco Antonio. *Historia de Guatemala o Recordacion Florida.* Madrid: L. Navarro, 1882–1883.

Furst, Peter. "Jaguar Baby or Toad Mother: A New Look at an Old Problem in Olmec Iconography." In *The Olmec and Their Neighbors.* Edited by Elizabeth P. Bensen. Washington D.C.: Dumbarton Oaks, 1981.

García Bacca, Juan D. "Comentarios a La Esencia de la Poesía de Heidegger." In *Revista Nacional de Cultura,* nos. 112–13 (1955).

Ginsberg, Allen. *Howl.* San Francisco: City Lights Books, 1956.

Glass, John B., "A Survey of Native Middle American Pictorial Manuscripts." In *The Handbook of Middle American Indians,* vol. 14, part 3. Edited by Howard Cline. Austin: University of Texas Press, 1975.

Glass, John B., and Donald Robertson. "A Census of Native Middle American Pictorial Manuscripts." In *The Handbook of Middle American Indians,* vol. 14, part 3. Edited by Howard Cline. Austin: University of Texas Press, 1975.

de Herrera y Tordesillas, Antonio. *Historia de las Indias Occidentales*. Madrid: Libreria del la Publicidad, 1854.

Hoffman, Albert. *LSD, My Problem Child: Reflections on Sacred Drugs, Mysticism, and Science*. Los Angeles: J. P. Tarcher, 1983.

Hunt, Eva. *The Transformation of the Hummingbird: Cultural Roots of a Zinacantecan Mythical Poem*. Ithaca, N.Y.: Cornell University Press, 1977.

Hurtak, J. J. *The Keys of Enoch*. Los Gatos, Calif.: The Academy for Future Science, 1977.

Huxley, Aldous. Introduction to *The Song of God, Bhagavad-Gita*. Translated by Swami Prabhavananda and Christopher Isherwood. New York: New American Library, 1954.

Jenkins, John Major. *Journey to the Mayan Underworld*. Boulder, Colo.: Four Ahau Press, 1989.

———. *7 Wind: A Quiché Maya Calendar for 1994*. Boulder, Colo.: Four Ahau Press, 1993.

———. *Tzolkin: Visionary Perspectives and Calendar Studies*. Garberville, Calif.: Borderland Sciences Research Foundation, 1994.

———. *Mayan Sacred Science*. Boulder, Colo.: Four Ahau Press, 1994, 2000.

———. *Maya Cosmogenesis 2012: The True Meaning of the Maya Calendar End Date*. Rochester, Vt.: Bear and Company, 1998.

———. *Metaphysical Speculations: Collected Poetry: 1982–1998*. Boulder, Colo.: Four Ahau Press, 1998.

Jonas, Hans. *The Gnostic Religion: The Message of the Alien God and the Beginnings of Christianity*, 2nd edition. Boston: Beacon Press, 1991.

Karttunen, Frances. *An Analytical Dictionary of Nahuatl*. Austin: University of Texas Press, 1983.

Kaufman, Bob. *The Ancient Rain: Poems 1956–1978*. New York, New Directions, 1981.

Kerouac, Jack. *On the Road*. New York: Signet Books, 1958.

Kolemainen, John. *Epic of the North: The Story of Finland's Kalevala*. New York Mills, Minn.: Northwestern Press, 1973.

Lawlor, Robert. *Sacred Geometry: Its Philosophy and Practice*. London: Thames and Hudson, 1987.

Lee, Peter. *The Big Smoke: The Chinese Art and Craft of Opium*. Thailand: Lamplight Books, 1999.

León-Portilla, Miguel. *Aztec Thought and Culture: A Study of the Ancient Nahuatl Mind.* Norman: University of Oklahoma Press, 1963.

Magnus, Albertus. *Grimoirium Verum.* English translation of the 1517 edition. www.hermetics.org/pdf/Grimoirium_Verum.pdf.

Matz, Marty. *Time Waits: Selected Poems 1956–1986.* San Francisco: JMF Publishing, 1987.

———. *Pipe Dreams.* Denver, Colo.: Four Ahau Press, 2000.

———. *A Sky of Fractured Feathers* (CD). New York: Fang Records, 2001.

———. *Pipe Dreams* (CD). New York: Fang Records, 2003.

Miller, Carol, and Guadalupe Rivera. *The Winged Prophet From Hermes to Quetzalcoatl: An Introduction to Mesoamerican Deities through the Tarot.* New York: Samuel Weiser, 1994.

Miller, Mary Ellen, and Karl A. Taube. *The Gods and Symbols of Ancient Mexico and the Maya: An Illustrated Dictionary of Mesoamerican Religion.* New York: Thames and Hudson, 1993.

Myerhoff, Barbara. *Peyote Hunt: The Sacred Journey of the Huichol Indians.* Ithaca: Cornell University Press, 1974.

Nasr, Seyyed Hossein. *Knowledge and the Sacred.* Albany: State University of New York Press, 1989.

Nicholson, Henry B. "Religion in Pre-Hispanic Central Mexico." In *The Handbook of Middle American Indians,* vol. 10. Austin: University of Texas Press, 1971.

Ouspensky, P. D. *In Search of the Miraculous: Fragments of An Unknown Teaching.* London: HBJ Publishers, 1949.

Plato. *Timaeus.* Edited by R. G. Bury. London: Loeb Classical Library, 1929.

Poimandres. In Hans Jonas, *The Gnostic Religion.*

Paz, Octavio. *Configurations.* New York: New Directions, 1971.

Richards, Roger. "Marty Matz: Falstaff in Leather Stetson and Vest." www.EastVillagePoetry.com, 2002.

Rose, Sharron. *Awakening the Feminine.* Three-part video series. Buellton, Calif.: Sacred Mysteries Video, 2001.

———. *The Path of the Priestess: A Guidebook for Awakening the Divine Feminine.* Rochester, Vt.: Inner Traditions, 2002.

de Sahagún, Bernardino. *A History of Ancient Mexico: The Religion and Ceremonies of the Aztec Indians.* Glorieta, N. M.: Rio Grande Press, 1976.

Schwaller de Lubicz, R. A. *Sacred Science*. Rochester, Vt.: Inner Traditions, 1982.

Scofield, Bruce. *Signs of Time: An Introduction to Mesoamerican Astrology*. Amherst, Mass.: One Reed Publications, 1994.

Seneca. *Naturales Quaestiones*. Edited by T. H. Corcoran. London: Loeb Classical Library, 1971.

Shearer, Tony. *Lord of the Dawn: Quetzalcoat and the Tree of Life*. Healdsburg, Calif.: Naturegraph, 1971.

———. *Beneath the Moon and Under the Sun*. Albuquerque, N. M.: Sun Publishing, 1975.

Silberman, Neil Asher. *Heavenly Powers: Unraveling the Secret History of the Kabbalah*. Edison, N. J.: Castle Books, 2000.

Soustelle, Jacques. *La Vie Quotidienne de Aztèques à la Veille de la Conquête Espagnole*, Paris: Librairie Hachtte, 1955.

Tedlock, Barbara. *Time and the Highland Maya*. Albuquerque: University of New Mexico Press, 1982.

Tedlock, Dennis, trans. *The Popol Vuh: The Definitive Edition of the Mayan Book of the Dawn of Life and the Glories of Gods and Kings*. New York: Simon and Shuster, 1996.

———. *Breath on the Mirror: Mythic Voices and Visions of the Living Maya*. San Francisco: Harper San Francisco, 1993.

Vazakas, Laki. "Remembering Marty Matz." In *Polarity eMagazine*, www.poem-beat.com/current/laki_vazakas.html, 2000.

Volguine, Alexandre. *Astrology of the Mayas and Aztecs*. Kent, England: Pythagorean Publications, 1969.

Walters, Derek. *Fortune-Telling by Mah Jongg: A Practical Guide to Divination Using the Ancient Chinese Game of Mah Jongg*. Wellingborough, England: Aquarian Press, 1987.

Waters, Frank. *Mexico Mystique: The Coming Sixth World of Consciousness*. Chicago: Sage Books, 1975.

Wilhelm, Richard. *The Secret of the Golden Flower*. Translated by C. F. Baynes. Commentary by Carl Jung. New York: Harcourt, Brace, Jovanovich, 1962.

Index

Note: Page numbers in italics refer to the novella *The Pyramid of Fire* (chapter 3).

Books of Related Interest

Galactic Alignment
The Transformation of Consciousness
According to Mayan, Egyptian, and Vedic Traditions
by John Major Jenkins

Maya Cosmogenesis 2012
The True Meaning of the Maya Calendar End-Date
by John Major Jenkins

The Mayan Calendar and the Transformation of Consciousness
by Carl Johan Calleman, Ph.D.
Foreword by José Argüelles

The Mayan Factor
Path Beyond Technology
by José Argüelles

The Mayan Oracle
Return Path to the Stars
by Ariel Spilsbury and Michael Bryner

Return of the Children of Light
Incan and Mayan Prophecies for a New World
by Judith Bluestone Polich

The Mysteries of the Great Cross of Hendaye
Alchemy and the End of Time
by Jay Weidner and Vincent Bridges

Secrets of Mayan Science/Religion
by Hunbatz Men

INNER TRADITIONS • BEAR & COMPANY
P.O. Box 388
Rochester, VT 05767
1-800-246-8648
www.InnerTraditions.com

Or contact your local bookseller